Pretty Good Number One

PRETTY GOOD NUMBER ONE
An American Family Eats Tokyo

MATTHEW AMSTER-BURTON

prettygoodnumberone.com

Cover by CL Smith
Book design by Matthew Amster-Burton
Text is set in Minion, Hiroshige, and Hiragino Mincho.

Publisher's Cataloging-in-Publication data

Amster-Burton, Matthew, 1975–

    Pretty Good Number One: An American Family Eats
Tokyo / Matthew Amster-Burton

    239 p. ; 22 cm
    Includes bibliographical references
    ISBN 978-1-4841269-8-1 (pbk.)

1. Dinners and Dining—Japan—Tokyo. 2. Food Writers—
Japan—Tokyo—Anecdotes. 3. Tokyo (Japan)—Description
and Travel   I. Title

DS896.38 .A478 2013
915.2135—dc23

To Iris

Contents

目次

On Japanese Words

日本語

THIS BOOK CONTAINS JAPANESE WORDS. Some are written in Japanese characters, but most are written in roman characters for the benefit of English speakers.

Japanese pronunciation is not terribly difficult for English speakers, but there are a couple of rules to keep in mind. An e at the end of a word is never silent, and is pronounced approximately like "eh" as in "bed." The restaurant Tamahide is pronounced "ta-ma-hee-deh." And g's are always hard as in "goat," not soft as in "gentle."

Introduction

序論

That first fleeting taste of Japan felt like the answer to some unspoken question.
—Pico Iyer

THE DIRECTIONS TO OUR APARTMENT begin like this:

Go out the north exit of Nakano Station and into the Sun Mall shopping arcade. After a few steps, you'll see Gindaco, the *takoyaki* (octopus balls) chain. Turn right into Pretty Good #1 Alley. Walk past the deli that specializes in *okowa* (steamed sticky rice with tasty bits), a couple of ramen shops, and a fugu restaurant. Go past the pachinko parlor, the grilled eel stand, the camera shops, and the stairs leading to Ginza Renoir coffee shop. If you see the bicycle parking lot in front of Life Supermarket, you're going the right way.

During this two-block walk through a typical neighborhood, you've passed more good food than in most midsized Western cities, even if you don't love octopus balls as much as I do.

Welcome to Tokyo.

Tokyo is unreal. It's the amped-up, neon-spewing cyber-city of literature and film. It's an alley teeming with fragrant grilled chicken shops. It's children playing safely in the street and riding the train across town with no parents in sight. It's a doughnut chain with higher standards of customer service than most high-end restaurants in America. A colossal meg-acity devoid of crime, grime, and bad food? Sounds more like a utopian novel than an earthly metropolis.

But Tokyo is real, and it is so unlikely, even up close, that it is *magic*. I hate it when people toss around words like "magic," but I spent a month in Tokyo in July 2012 in a tiny apart-ment with my wife, Laurie, and our eight-year-old daughter, Iris, and calling the experience anything other than magical would be dishonest.

Tokyo is not a beautiful place, but it metes out its charms with almost scientific regularity. Every time one of us went for a walk, we came back with exciting news: a peculiar old building, a funny sign, a family of cats, a new kind of yo-gurt-flavored candy. Yes, Iris went out often for unaccompa-nied walks; to my knowledge, she was never forced to join the *yakuza*, although she occasionally came back with a sus-picious tattoo.

Good food is so easy to find in Tokyo that the city itself seems like a restaurant. In over a month, we had *one meal* that I found disappointing, and it wasn't actually bad, just bland.

We also had meals, many of them at quirky, inexpensive neighborhood restaurants, that were so great that thinking about them buries the needle on my nostalgia meter. Tokyo provokes a sentimental homesickness in me that I've never felt about any other place. It's embarrassing, and I like it.

The Tokyo train map looks like a bowl of DayGlo ramen, but we felt like experts within days. Our apartment was one stop away from Shinjuku Station, the world's busiest train station. Sounds like hell, doesn't it? Well, Shinjuku is nice. Sure, it's teeming with the purposeful strides of people trying to get somewhere else, but finding your train is easy, and getting carried along in the flood of commuters is the urban equivalent of inner tubing on a lazy river.

In short, Tokyo is the opposite of the DMV: it's the least annoying place I've ever been.

Despite these charms, there is a strange lack of swooning travel memoirs about Tokyo. If Westerners think of Tokyo at all, it's as the capital of a nation struggling to right itself after years of economic stagnation capped by a devastating earthquake and nuclear disaster. Even before the Tōhoku quake, however, Tokyo was a slightly off-the-map tourist destination. How many Tokyo tourist attractions can you name offhand? I'm going to guess zero. If you said Ginza or the Imperial Palace, put down your *Lonely Planet* and quit cheating.

But think about Paris for a moment: its warrens of narrow streets, perfect for strolling and getting happily lost; its modern transportation system; its museums and monuments; its world-class shopping; and above all its food and drink, irresistible from breakfast to dinner, from Michelin-starred palaces to hole-in-the-wall crepe shops.

Tokyo has all of the above, including more Michelin stars than Paris. And there's no shortage of Tokyo guidebooks and blogs, plus books by Westerners who go to Kyoto (never Tokyo) to find themselves. But the city is missing the English-language books that catapult Paris into the imagination of every romantic. This book is my small attempt to fill that gap.

My friend Becky likes to talk about Vacation Head, a common traveler's malady that causes a person to fall madly in love with a destination and overlook all its faults. My relationship with Tokyo developed under a scorching case of Vacation Head. There is no dark underbelly to be found here (just lots of pork belly), but I think mine is a perfectly valid perspective. For one thing, nothing is stopping you from having your own torrid and shallow affair with Tokyo. For another, I've suffered many attacks of Vacation Head, but this one made every prior case feel like a bad one-night stand. Something is *different* about Tokyo.

Iris was born in 2003, and by the time she was two, it was clear that we had two things in common: a fondness for naps and an appreciation for sushi and other Japanese food, which Laurie did not share. I was a stay-at-home dad with a kid who demanded endless made-up stories, so one day, instead of continuing her favorite epic tale of talking dogs, I told her about a place called Tokyo. I'd never been there and knew little about it other than that it was probably a good place to find some of our favorite foods. Maybe some day we could go there together, just the two of us. In other words, we formed a conspiracy.

We talked about it nearly every day on the way to preschool in the morning. Preschool was ten blocks away, and Iris was so small at first that I pushed her there in the stroller, and we would talk about going to an amusement park and eating conveyor belt sushi and Beard Papa cream puffs. My dad liked to ask Iris, "What are you going to do in Japan?" and then laugh when she said, "Go to an amusement park and eat cream puffs."

In my book *Hungry Monkey,* which I wrote when Iris was four, I revealed that we were planning the trip:

> Iris and I will eat at a skeezy yakitori joint and enjoy char-grilled chicken parts on a stick. We'll go to an eel restaurant and eat several courses of eel, my favorite fish. Iris's favorite is mackerel, so we'll also eat plenty of salt-broiled mackerel, *saba no shioyaki,* tearing off fatty bits with our chopsticks. We will eat our weight in rice…we'll have breakfast at Tsukiji, the world's largest fish market. And we'll eat plenty of sushi from a conveyor belt.

We set aside a hundred bucks each month into a savings account, and eventually the trip started to change from something to talk about on the way to school into something that could actually happen. Then, when Iris was six, we did it, just the two of us: we spent six days in Japan.

We never went to the cream puff place. We didn't eat any conveyor belt sushi or salt-broiled mackerel. We didn't go to an eel restaurant or eat breakfast at the fish market. We did go to a skeezy yakitori place, however, which is where Iris discovered *bonjiri,* chicken tail, the fattiest, juiciest bit of the chicken, and the best to grill on a stick and brush with sweetened soy sauce.

In short, we barely did any of the things we originally planned to do, and it was the best vacation ever. Japan is absurdly welcoming and easy to navigate. Having a six-year-old along turned out to be an asset; Iris made a good ambassador, and the trip was delightfully free of the miscommunications that tend to crop up between otherwise amiable adults under the stress of travel.

Something about Tokyo's exuberant modernism made Iris and me feel like the city existed just to make us happy: *Cheer up!* the waving *maneki-neko* cats seemed to whisper. *You're in Tokyo!*

Iris and I came back with a list of Tokyo attractions we never made it to on our first trip, a list about a month long. And we started to drive Laurie insane by breaking into misty-eyed reminiscences about our cherry blossom days in Japan.

"Fine," said Laurie. "If Tokyo is so great, let's all get an apartment there and stay for a month." Probably she was thinking:

- "This idea is so obviously unaffordable that Matthew, the notorious cheapskate, will dismiss it immediately."
- "Let's see how much they like Japan after spending a month in a tiny apartment living like newly landed immigrants."

Challenge accepted!

One other guy accompanied us that summer. I apologize, because I kind of wish I could get rid of him, but he's proved hard to shake, like a case of mono.

His name is Shiro Yamaoka, and he is my literary alter ego. Shiro is a rat of an imaginary friend. He's a self-centered, lazy, know-it-all with unkempt hair.

Yamaoka is the hero of Oishinbo, a long-running *manga* comic series focused on Japanese cuisine. He's a daily newspaper reporter who'd rather sleep at his desk and daydream about fried gyoza than write articles. When the paper puts him in charge of the Ultimate Menu project, collecting essential dishes from the four corners of Japan, Shiro finds his calling, not to mention some office romance with fellow reporter Yuko Kurita. Kurita is Yamaoka's intellectual equal, his superior in social skills, and super foxy. I know someone like that.

Now, having said all this, Oishinbo is easy to criticize. The characters are thinner than *washi* paper, and the plots are absurd. Yamaoka is constantly dragging his entire office off to East Bumfuck, Japan, to learn about taro roots or whatever. He works out his daddy issues by challenging his estranged father, Kaibara Yūzan, to a series of Iron Chef–style culinary battles.

But you know what? *I'm also a one-dimensional character.* Probably this is a guy thing, but I've never had a complicated inner life. Shiro Yamaoka cares about good food and is intolerant of bad food, but he's also distrustful of anything with a gourmet pedigree. He is probably a good writer but takes the rest of the week off if he writes two whole articles. One reason he's drawn to the world of food is because he finds flavor and texture a lot easier to understand than human behavior. If Yamaoka wrote a book, he wouldn't think twice about spending pages haranguing people to read his favorite comic.

Every character in Oishinbo is oddly obsessed with food. I'd assumed this was a literary device, but now I know otherwise. Everyone in Oishinbo is obsessed with food because they live in Tokyo, where great food is omnipresent and impossible to ignore.

And to drink? Japan makes great beer, coffee, sake, and liquor, but let's begin the way I start every day, in Tokyo or elsewhere, with a cup of green tea.

Tea

お茶

MOST AIRLINES SERVING ASIA HIGHLIGHT their standard of service, the comeliness of their flight attendants, or the culturally informed punctuality of their flights. But we chose an American airline that flies nonstop from Seattle to Tokyo and neither promises nor delivers anything special.

Even so, there is a tiny welcome-to-Japan moment on any flight to Japan when the flight attendant offers you a choice of "coffee or *ocha.*" The latter is green tea, and it is doubly comforting when offered by a flight attendant with a hint of a Texas twang.

Japanese tea is weird. Laurie, who drinks English-style black tea with milk, absolutely hates it. My mother thinks the tea leaves smell like spinach, and I can't deny it. In most tea-drinking countries, the leaves are processed so that their origin as the green leaves of a plant is disguised. This is true even of Chinese green tea, which is wonderful in its own way but which always has a hint of smoky barbecue to it because the leaves are dried briefly over a fire.

In Japan, on the other hand, the greener the leaves the better. "Vegetal," a word which is never used as a compliment outside a mulch pile, is an apt descriptor for Japanese tea. Some Japanese teas are so green they look like FD&C dye was involved, and some have the texture of rich chicken stock and thousands of tiny green leaf flecks swirling in the cup. (Really, tea fans get excited about these qualities.)

And only Japan makes *matcha*, which is nothing more than high quality tea leaves, ground into powder and whipped up with hot water like a smoothie.

If the average person knows anything about Japanese tea, it's that it figures in a tea ceremony that visitors to Japan pretend to enjoy while sitting for hours with their legs in a position conducive to deep-vein thrombosis. Honestly, I'm not going to defend the tea ceremony, but *Japanese tea is a ceremony in a cup.* It is only ever itself: it's not easy to like, and you can't ease into it by hiding its flavor behind sweet or floral or fruity additives. Sure, these combinations exist, but they're terrible gateway drugs: a matcha latte drinker is still going to find pure matcha challenging. Like Edo-period Japan, Japanese tea walls itself off against foreign influences.

Predictably, perhaps, I've gravitated toward the form of Japanese tea with the funniest name: *fukamushi sencha*. All Japanese tea is steamed before drying; fukamushi is steamed a little longer. This makes for spindly little leaves, like pine needles ground underfoot, and a thick, rich, cloudy cup of tea. I can sense Laurie cringing already.

But I'm not picky: any Japanese tea will do, which is kind of like saying "any caviar will do." Japanese tea is virtually unknown in the United States. Starbucks doesn't serve it, except for an occasional sighting of matcha Frappuccinos in the summer. No major brand (not Stash, not Lipton, not Celestial Seasonings) sells it in bags. I buy it online from o-cha.com; in teabags for travel from Seattle's Uwajimaya supermarket; and hot, every morning, from my neighborhood tea cafe, Remedy Teas. Of all the snobby things I do—and it's not a short list—carrying teabags is among the worst. I can't help it. It's not just the caffeine: after a few days without a sip of Japanese tea, I start to think about it all the time.

So when I'm presented with a cup of ocha on the flight to Tokyo, it's an auspicious gesture, because in Japan, everyone drinks green tea all the time. Restaurants serve a bottomless free cup with meals. Hotel rooms provide an electric kettle and teabags. Tea shops sell a variety of types in beautiful 100-gram packets; you can spot a tea shop in Tokyo by looking for a giant green plastic ice cream cone advertising matcha soft-serve.

In 2010, I dragged Iris to a town called Uji because I wanted to go to a particular tea shop founded in 1160. Uji turned out to be a sleepy town devoted to temples and green tea and little else. We went to the tea shop and received free samples of *gyokuro,* the fanciest kind of brewed tea in Japan. Iris accepted her cup and managed to communicate, in one horrified look, *I know that good manners require me to take this cup, and if you tell me I have to drink it, too, I will literally die right here in this tea shop.* I drank her cup and mine, and it was great, and then we got lost and hungry trying to get back to the train station. Two years later, if I say the word "Uji," Iris glares like I'm talking about detention.

So in 2012, I went out for tea by myself, in Ginza. As you approach exit 7 from Ginza Station, the floors, walls, and ceiling transition from concrete and subway tile to sleek black stone. That's because exit 7 is also the entrance to an Armani store.

I was not, you will be shocked to learn, on my way to Armani; I was headed to Uogashi Meicha, a merely 75-year-old tea shop also known as Cha Ginza. Uogashi is fancy, but not Armani fancy. Wedged into three stories of a slim building on a Ginza side street, Uogashi is the perfect place for an introduction to Japanese tea and is one of my favorite places in Tokyo.

To have tea at Uogashi, you buy a ticket on the ground floor for either the second floor *sencha* cafe or the third floor matcha cafe. I bought a 700-yen ticket for the matcha cafe, and the woman at the counter warned me, "It's kind of...outside." No problem, I said: I brought my hat. It was not that kind of outside. It was a claustrophobic covered roof garden with a couple of modern sculptures that, on another day, I might have been moved to gaze at contemplatively. A fan hummed loudly but produced no ventilation.

The host asked if I wanted matcha or *kakigōri*. Kakigōri is flavored shave ice, a Japanese snow cone. I reasoned, stupidly, that I had not come all the way to Ginza to eat a snow cone, so I asked for matcha. As soon as I'd put in my order, the host started serving kakigōri to everyone else in the cafe, huge mounds of delicate shave ice topped with freshly whipped matcha, which patrons spooned up with evident delight. I tried to remember the Japanese word for "to change one's mind" and came up empty-headed. It was too late, anyway: the host brought me a cup of *koicha,* thick matcha, thicker than motor oil but much tastier. Only very good matcha can be used to make koicha; lesser tea will whip up chalky and bitter. I cradled my rustic tea bowl in two hands and tried to ignore the crunch of kakigōri on all sides.

It took me about three slurps to finish the koicha, leaving the tea bowl coated with an emerald film. The hostess traded my empty bowl for a perfect yuzu macaron and then asked me the most wonderful question: next up would be thin matcha (*usucha*), and did I want it hot or iced?

"*Aisu,*" I panted. The ice cubes in my cold matcha seemed to have been selected for artistic merit, a large central iceberg surrounded by four little shards, like a family of seals. I downed it quickly and thereby staved off heatstroke.

So what does matcha taste like, if you've never had it? It's commonly described as tasting "green," which is true, albeit begging the question. Good matcha is naturally very sweet, a plant sweetness quite unlike bad matcha sweetened with sugar, which is common in shelf-stable convenience store drinks and at coffee places. When you're drinking matcha, even high quality stuff, you can rub your tongue against the roof of your mouth and feel that it was whipped up from a powder. If you like the scent of newly mown grass, you would probably enjoy matcha. It's not much like brewed green tea at all.

Brewed tea is what you get on the *second* floor of Uogashi Meicha. On another day, I took my seat in that second-floor sencha cafe, and the other customers broke out into unrestrained giggles. What a convivial assembly tea engenders! Actually, I had parked my butt on the table, rather than the seat. This is a no-no, according to local customs. I moved aside to make room for a cup of gyokuro. Like matcha, gyokuro leaves are grown under shade for a couple of weeks before being harvested, and this makes the plant go crazy, producing barrels of chlorophyll to trap what little sun makes it through the gauzy canopy. This produces a vivid color and unusually intense flavor. Also unusually intense price tags. Gyokuro is brewed at a very low temperature for tea (140°F) and served in a tiny teacup.

I was just raising the gyokuro cup to my lips and hoping not to violate any more social norms when someone asked, "Do you like Japanese tea?" It was a young man sitting with a young woman just next to me. (Sitting on the seats, I should add.) They introduced themselves as Akira and Emi. They wanted to practice their English. I wanted to practice Japanese. I handed Akira my business card and he accepted it with two hands and looked it over carefully, exactly as described in every cultural guide for business travelers to Japan. The book added that it's considered extremely rude to fold or otherwise mistreat someone's business card.

Presumably this also means you're not supposed to laugh at someone's business card, but mine is ridiculous and incomprehensible, even to native English speakers, because it features the name of my blog (Roots and Grubs) and a quote from Iris that seemed really funny at the time. The more I tried to explain, the more we all laughed. Probably I should order some new business cards with a recognizable job title on them, but that would involve getting a job.

Like most young children, Iris is capable of making friends instantly. *You're approximately four feet tall? Great, let's hang out.* One of the great things about traveling to a foreign place (and I realize every traveler before me has observed this) is that it allows adults to make friends in the same way children do. When I meet a new person on my home turf, it's as if we're actively looking for reasons to dislike each other. *Sure, we can be friends, as long as you're not guilty of anything on my endless list of pet peeves.* I'm the *worst* about this. Is this starting to sound like a voiceover from *Sex and the City* yet?

In Tokyo, however, there was just no way for me to be overly judgmental. Akira and Emi and I all liked tea and foreign language practice and making fun of the guy who just put his ass on the tabletop. Lifelong friendships have been forged on a flimsier basis. We finished our tea and planned to meet again. I escaped the tea cafe without committing any other faux pas and ran home (well, took the Marunouchi line) to tell Laurie and Iris that I'd made some new friends. A couple of days later I got an email from Akira inviting me to meet him in Ueno for dinner.

In his book *Wrong About Japan*, Peter Carey takes his teenage son to Tokyo for a trip focused on anime and manga. For some reason—perhaps because writing about a brief family vacation didn't seem like sufficient material for a book— Carey gave his son an imaginary friend named Takashi, who popped up in every scene as needed and participated in every adventure, offering wise commentary.

Takashi seemed less fake after meeting Akira and Emi. Laurie, Iris, and I spent the kind of afternoons with them that could be edited into a hackneyed getting-to-know-you montage: strolling in the park, paddling in swan boats, eating ice cream, shopping in Ginza. Maybe we met the two nicest people in Tokyo. Or, as I always say: what a convivial assembly tea engenders.

West Side Living

中野

SINCE WE RETURNED FROM OUR trip, Iris has been telling everyone we know to visit Tokyo. "And you *have* to go to Nakano," she adds. At this, Laurie and I share a knowing glance. Iris is right that Nakano is lively, welcoming to visitors and children, overstuffed with great inexpensive food, and minutes from central Tokyo. There is also practically no reason for a tourist to go to Nakano, because all of these qualities apply to dozens if not hundreds of other neighborhoods.

The western suburbs of Tokyo stretch endlessly along the Chūō train line until they reach the slopes of Mount Takao, more than thirty miles from central Tokyo. Nakano, one stop from Shinjuku on the rapid train, is an inner suburb, and that's where we rented our tiny apartment.

Nakano is full of great, cheap restaurants, both chains and independents. The ubiquity of great food in Tokyo is beyond imagination. It's not just that I'm interested in food and pay close attention to restaurants and takeout shops, although that's true. In Tokyo, great food really is in your face, all the time: sushi, yakitori, Korean barbecue, eel, tempura, *tonkatsu*, bento shops, delis, burgers (Western and Japanese-style), the Japanese take on Western food called *yōshoku*, and, most of all, noodles. I found this cheap everyday food—lovingly called *B-kyū* ("B-grade") by its fans—so satisfying and so easy on the wallet that I rarely ventured into anything you might call a nice restaurant.

World-class foreign food exists in Tokyo, but you're not going to just stumble into it. In Nakano, we saw a pizza place, a Thai restaurant, an Indian restaurant, a juice bar called Kale Juice Shop, and a few Chinese restaurants. It was nothing like the profusion of international food you'd find in any neighborhood in New York. If you love Japanese food, you're going to love Tokyo.

We live in a good food neighborhood in Seattle called Capitol Hill, but compared to Nakano, it's a food desert like you hear about on NPR. I blew a whole hour theorizing about what aspect of the Japanese or American character could explain the difference before realizing that it's just a numbers game. Nakano and Capitol Hill are almost exactly the same size in land area. But Nakano has *eight times the population.* That means a lot of hungry mouths. I enjoy sharing this statistic with my Seattle NIMBY neighbors who grumble about how our neighborhood has too many people already. Nakano doesn't feel overcrowded; it feels *alive.*

If a Tokyoite knows anything about Nakano, it's likely to

be Nakano Broadway, a shopping mall with several floors devoted to Japanese comics (manga) and animation (anime). It is geek central. I found most of it incomprehensible, but I did enjoy browsing at Junkworld, which sells useful electronic discards, like old working digital cameras for $5 and assorted connectors and dongles and sound cards. In the 1980s, when William Gibson was padding around the streets of Tokyo and inventing the world of *Neuromancer,* Japan was the place where the future had already arrived, where you could find electronic toys that wouldn't hit American shelves for years, if ever. For a variety of reasons (blogs and online shopping, advances in international shipping, the fact that the coolest mobile phones are now designed in Silicon Valley and Seoul), this is no longer true. While it's still fun to go to Akihabara at night and shop all seven floors of a neon-lit electronics superstore, you won't bring home any objects of nerdy wet dreams.

Two areas where Japanese consumer electronics are still the undisputed world champs are cameras and toilets. I mean, not combined into the same device, as far as I know. But I do find it odd that the U.S., which devotes so much GDP to personal comfort, has really boring toilets. We sat on toilets with heated seats; toilets with a hand-washing sink on top of the tank that goes on automatically upon flushing; toilets with spray nozzles pointed in assorted directions. "Who would use the bidet function in a public bathroom?" asked Laurie rhetorically. I shuffled my feet and said nothing.

Americans have a curious relationship with housing. We like our houses the way we like our action movie stars: big, well-dressed, and approachable. We like wall-to-wall carpeting and master bedroom suites, three-car garages and double-sink bathrooms.

A Tokyo apartment is unlike the Better Homes and Gardens image of the good life in the same way a gecko is unlike a *T. rex*.

Tokyo apartment listings don't use the "2 bedroom/1 bath" terminology common in the United States, because bedrooms are converted to living rooms during the day and evening. It would be crazy to waste a whole room by using it only for sleeping. Our second-floor apartment in Nakano was a 1DK: 1 room plus dining room and kitchen. (The kitchen and dining room are, of course, really just one room.)

A typical family of three in Tokyo isn't crammed into such a small space, although some certainly are. As of the 2008 census, the average household in Tokyo had 2.2 members and about 300 square feet per person. Our entire apartment was 260 square feet.

Americans who move out of their parents' house and into a college dorm love every filthy square foot of the place and then, once they graduate, leave the small-space life behind as soon as they can (with perhaps a wistful copy of *The Not So Big House* on the coffee table). I've always prided myself on being a small-space guy and kept using the term "McMansion" long after every other intolerable hipster stopped saying it, but after we reserved the apartment in Nakano, I had a total freakout: *Oh, shit. This apartment is 260 square feet. We are going to kill and eat each other, sashimi-style, by week two. This trip was a stupid, stupid idea. Hmm, if someone has to be eaten as sashimi, maybe at least we can serve them with fresh wasabi.*

Naturally, life in the apartment turned out to be downright relaxing.

At the entrance to our apartment is the *genkan,* where you remove your shoes. The genkan is just a tiny square of floor with a single step up to the kitchen to mark the beginning of the no-shoes area. There's a shoe cabinet in the genkan, and Iris often needled me for putting my shoes in the same drawer as hers, because of shoe cooties. I wonder whether anyone has spent time in Japan and returned to the West without internalizing the belief that the soles of shoes accumulate every sort of ill, physical and spiritual, and that you'd no more wear shoes into a person's house than piss on their rug.

Many houses and apartments in Japan feature one or more tatami rooms. Ours did not, but I'd like to say a few words about tatami anyway, because they are cool. Tatami are rectangular straw mats used as flooring. You've probably seen them at a Japanese restaurant. If your room has tatami flooring, you roll out your futon in the evening and go to sleep, then fold up the futon and put it away in a closet during the day. You hang your futon regularly from the balcony railing to air out using a special clip designed for this purpose.

Yes, every apartment in Tokyo has a balcony. Without one, where would you hang your clothes to dry? You certainly don't have a clothes dryer, which are almost unheard of in Tokyo. Our washing machine, a small top-loading model, sat on the balcony and sprayed rinse water directly out the back of the machine, where it cascaded across the ledge, into a drainpipe, and onto the ground. We were worried that a hose wasn't hooked up until we looked across and saw our neighbor's washer doing the same thing.

Every night, we put down the sofa bed, laid out Iris's futon, and hauled the coffee table into the kitchen. In the morning, we reversed the process. That coffee table and its movers got quite a workout.

The living room was air-conditioned, well lit, and great for snacking, for watching sumo on TV, for lazing around, and for reading the Japan Times (one of the English-language newspapers). I enjoyed the Japan Times very much, especially the TV listings. "Items presented for evaluation include...a piece of pottery linked to the Shimazu fief of Kagoshima," went the teaser for a program called *Family Treasure Appraisers*. Actually, I know just as much about the Shimazu fief of Kagoshima as I do about anything the appraisers talk about on *Antiques Roadshow* (i.e., zilch).

At night, we stretched out on our futon and converted sofa, and as Iris wavered on the edge of sleep, she'd entertain us by trying to make us guess which words she was surrounding with air quotes in the darkness. This is not as hard as it sounds.

"In the wet, hot depths of a Japanese summer even the slightly built, lightly clad Japanese suffer. It is a period that has to be endured. Summer is the most demoralizing season in Japan. The best thing to do, if one can, is simply to sit still in a matted room, clay-walled, with the shoji slid open on the shady side of a small, water-rilled stone garden sprited with green bamboos,

and to do nothing.
   —James Kirkup, *Japan Behind the Fan*

Shortly before the trip, I had tea with my friend Tara Austen Weaver, who lived in Japan for years. I was excited about having my own miniature Japanese kitchen and asked her what seasonal delights she would cook up if she were living in Japan in the summer.

"Nothing," she replied without hesitation.

James Kirkup and Tara Weaver are right: July weather in Japan is odious. Kirkup, however, was writing in the 1960s, and Tara lived in a rural area with few modern conveniences. For Kirkup's clay-walled room, I would substitute an air-conditioned apartment or perhaps the second floor of the Starbucks on Nakano-dōri. It's disappointing that Japan has not yet invented a supercooled summer jumpsuit, but it's only a matter of time. It could be lined with slender ice packs and stored in the freezer.

As for the cooking, well, I admit it: weather and the ubiquity of great, cheap restaurants sidelined my grand plans to cook my way through the Japanese repertoire. As the saying goes, why buy the octopus when you can get the takoyaki for free?

Still, it was a nice little kitchen, a strip along the wall of the dining room. To the left of the sink was a stack of appliances: refrigerator, microwave, toaster oven. Printed on the front of the microwave was a quick guide to heating times for the four items you're most likely to heat up: rice, sake, milk, and bento boxes.

Nearly every family in Japan has a version of the same stove, two gas burners and a fish grill. A more luxurious model might have three or four burners, but for a small apartment, two is plenty. Before the advent of the gas stove, the Japanese home had a *kamado,* an imposing charcoal-fueled stove with cooking vessels sunk into a rangetop, each topped with a wooden lid sporting fin-like handles. The kamado has been reborn in the form of the Big Green Egg and similar ceramic barbecue devices. The Big Green Egg has a big green advantage over the classic kamado: *you're not burning charcoal inside your house.*

But back to the modern stove. A few years ago, the New York Times caused a minor stir by publishing a photo of columnist Mark Bittman cooking at home. Bittman is the best-selling author of many enormous cookbooks (*How to Cook Everything, How to Cook Everything Vegetarian, Mark Bittman Forgot More Recipes Than You Ever Knew,* etc.), and his home kitchen is a classic Manhattan apartment afterthought.

"People like to cook when they're camping and in other places where the situation is less than adequate," Bittman said at the time. "For some reason they think they have to have a great kitchen to cook at home, but it's not true."

So far Bittman and the average Japanese home cook are on the same page. But then he added, "One of the things I hate about my stove is you can't put four pots on it at the same time, so you cook with two pots and use the oven more."

Boohoo! The only oven in a Japanese kitchen is a toaster oven. If you want something baked or roasted, you buy it at a shop.

The fish grill is a clever little device. When I was a kid, I hung out with a friend who had a weird uncle. Not sleazy weird, just eccentric. The most obvious mark of his eccentricity, aside from his seventies mustache, was that he liked to cook his dinner in the broiler at the bottom of the gas range. He'd be on the floor, opening the little drawer and peering at his piece of meat or whatever. I don't think I saw a broiler drawer between 1990 and 2012, but the Japanese fish grill is the same thing in miniature: a drip pan with a metal grate on top, which you slide under a gas flame.

Several people in Tokyo told me they never use their fish grill, as if the reason for this would be evident, but I found that it worked great, especially for juicy, hard-to-overcook fish like mackerel, the most common (and cheapest) fish in Japanese supermarkets. I'd lean over and slide the drawer out to check on my fish, just like the weird uncle. My mustache is more groomed, but not by much.

Later, I discovered the problem with the fish grill, in three steps:

1. Present your family with succulent grilled fish. (Did I mention that, for some reason, broiling is always known as "grilling" in Japan?)
2. Slide the fish grill shut so that no one takes a blow to the kidney while walking through the kitchen.
3. Three days later, open the fish grill and scream. Surprise! Rancid, congealed fish grease.

Japanese cuisine has a small footprint. Home cooks have

been preparing it in tiny kitchens for generations. Some of the best parts of a Japanese meal, such as the pickles, just sit around waiting to be eaten. The same goes for rice: everyone has a rice cooker, and at any time of day it tends to be on the KEEP WARM setting, full of cooked rice. While the two burners of the stove are occupied, the rice cooker sits quietly in the corner and treats your rice with the proper respect.

For my first home-cooked meal in Tokyo, I took an assortment of beautiful Japanese ingredients and did what came naturally: I made Chinese food. I stir-fried some beautifully marbled *kurobuta* (Berkshire breed) pork with bok choy, ginger, and leeks, sauced it with soy sauce, mirin, and vinegar, and served it over rice, sprinkled with *shichimi tōgarashi* seven-spice mixture. This seemed like a reasonable act of Japanese-Chinese fusion. I made some quick-pickled cucumbers on the side. This was before we discovered that anything you do to a Japanese cucumber diminishes it. I should have known this; once I interviewed a Japanese-American farmer who grows more than a hundred Asian vegetables in Washington state. Naturally, I asked him about his personal favorite. Cucumber, he said.

"How do you prepare it?" I asked.

"Slice and eat."

The whole meal was about the same as something I'd make at home, but I cooked it in Japan. It was like the SpongeBob SquarePants episode where SpongeBob has to work the night shift at the Krusty Krab, and he keeps saying things like, "I'm chopping lettuce...at night!" I was slicing cucumbers...in Tokyo!

When we moved in, our landlord, Mac, handed us an official four-page color guide explaining how to sort our garbage. "Even Japanese people have trouble," he said. "Hang in there." He flashed the thumbs-up. Then he walked off into the Nakano sun, leaving us alone with this document; it was like being a new parent all over again.

I'd heard people complain about the byzantine rules of Tokyo garbage and recycling, but honestly, I had no idea. In Seattle, we sort our discards into three categories: recycling, compost, and other. The first two categories go on to theoretically productive reuse, and those unredeemables in the last category go to the landfill. I've grumbled about Seattle trash policy in the past; I will never do so again.

In Tokyo, there are five main categories of trash, with multiple subcategories and exceptions. Each category is collected only on certain days. The apartment manager puts out the proper cans on the proper days, and if you don't take the stuff out in time, it's like missing a ferry, only smellier.

The catchall category is Combustible waste, meaning stuff that should go to the incinerator: food scraps, nonrecyclable plastic, diapers, small yard waste ("pruned brunches," according to the guide). The existence of this category led to many iterations of the following conversation:

MATTHEW: Is this Combustible?

LAURIE: No, I think it's Plastic.

MATTHEW: Everything is combustible if you get it hot enough. That's just physics.

Plastic is not just any plastic. It has to be recyclable and clean without food stains. It is your responsibility as a citizen to make a good-faith effort to wash food residues (say, takoyaki grease) off the plastic before putting it in the Plastic bin. It took me a couple of weeks to realize that there's a Plastic recycling symbol. It looks like the first two syllables of "purasuchikku" written in katakana. You're welcome.

Oh, but wait. Not all plastic is Plastic. PET bottles go in a separate bin and are collected on a separate day. Summer in Tokyo is high season for drink vending machines, which are so common it's as if they're following you. Don't tell any of our environmentally sensitive friends in Seattle, but we probably went through 250 PET bottles over the course of the month. There's more than one way to recycle a PET bottle: our friend Akira built a raft out of them.

Paper is the worst. You're supposed to bundle your newspapers and then slip small pieces of paper (shopping lists, unwanted love notes) in between the newspapers. These parcels are then tied up and placed at group collection points for collection by "voluntary community groups." Laurie somehow figured out not only where and when to put out Paper, but also which type of string to bind it with. I asked her how she did this, because it seemed like sorcery. "I figured it out by watching the streets," she replied, which is exactly how I learned to rap.

Thermal receipt paper goes in Combustibles, not Paper. No transaction in Tokyo is finished without a receipt. I would not be at all surprised to learn that hookers give receipts.

Noncombustibles are mainly metal things. By keeping an eye out for the Plastic symbol, I learned just how many things in life appear to be metal but are actually plastic. This struck me as deeply metaphorical.

Is there more to it than this? you might be wondering. Oh yes, there is. Page 3 of the handout (you are referring to your handout, right?) displays a massive chart of Frequently Asked Items. Some are easy. Aluminum foil? Noncombustible. Stuffed doll 30cm or smaller (Beanie Babies)? Combustible. Larger than 30cm (Cabbage Patch Kids)? Special large item pickup; call ahead.

The frequently asked list has 112 items. One of them, and this is not a joke, is *sphygmomanometer.* If you must know, it's Noncombustible but must be put in a separate bag and labeled. Do you know how to say "sphygmomanometer" in Japanese? I barely know how to say it in English.

Eventually, I did get the hang of garbage sorting, and I went around humming a little song about Combustibles. It took until the end of the month to figure out a solution to another form of useless cruft, small change.

In Japan, cash is still king. Credit and debit card payments are rare, and I never saw one person pay with a cell phone. Back home in Seattle, I'm a debit card devotee, but in Tokyo, I was constantly fumbling with coins and bills, and that's what you'd find on top of our shoe cabinet: a yogurt container overflowing with 1-yen coins, plus many precarious stacks of 10- and 5-yen coins.

The 1-yen coins are the worst—worse than pennies. They're made of aluminum and weigh practically nothing (1 gram, to be exact). They feel like play money.

Japanese currency is just different enough from American to drive me nuts. One yen is equivalent to about 1 U.S. cent.

There are 10,000-, 5000-, and 1000-yen bills, equivalent to $100s, $50s, and $10s. ATMs in Tokyo—at least the 7-Eleven ATMs that accepted my American ATM card—dispense only the largest 10,000-yen bills, and every merchant is happy to break a Benjamin. Actually, the 10,000-yen bill features the stern visage of Japanese enlightenment figure Yukichi Fukuzawa. I have no idea whether anyone calls the bills Fukuzawas, but I like the sound of it.

So the bills are easy. The problem is the coins. Japan issues 500- and 100-yen coins, worth about $5 and $1, respectively. In the U.S., it's easy to distinguish between real money and chump change: real money folds. If you get a hole in your pocket in Indiana and all your change falls into a sewer grate, big deal. In Japan, it's easy to end up carrying $25 worth of change, particularly if you come from the U.S. and automatically reach for bills whenever you're making a nontrivial purchase.

To make matters worse, there is no tipping in Japan. One day, I went to a very fancy tofu restaurant for lunch. The service was, of course, fabulous. At the end of the meal I paid exactly the amount shown on the bill, which was close to $100. If I'd tried to leave even an extra 100 yen on the table, I know exactly what would have happened: a waitress would have run after me to tell me I forgot some money.

If I were living in Japan long-term, I'd develop a coin-management strategy. I asked our friend Kate, who lives in Chiba, what she does with her coin hoard. "I spend it," she said. Both cashiers and the people in line behind you are very understanding if you want to count out exact change. Or if they're grumbling internally, they do an amazing job of hiding it. Kate also mentioned that it's considered good luck to keep a 5-yen piece, which has a hole in the middle, in your pocket. The 5-yen is also the only piece of Japanese money with no Arabic numerals on it, so you see foreigners squinting at them a lot.

So how did we eventually rid ourselves of those coins? We spent them at a cat cafe.

Millions of Tokyoites find themselves in the same position as Iris. They love cats but aren't allowed to have a cat at home. In Iris's case, it's because her parents are *so* unfair. We are unfair, in part, because we remember the time we cat-sat for a friend's purebred Siberian for a weekend at our apartment, and the cat meowed all night and attacked our feet.

At some point, we'll probably give in. But Tokyo offers cat cafes, a commercial solution to the problem of wanting to commune with cats but being unwilling or unable to have one at home.

Iris's favorite cat cafe is Nekorobi, in the Ikebukuro neighborhood. When I first heard about cat cafes, I imagined something like Starbucks with a cat on your lap. Wrong. Nekorobi is what you'd get if you asked a cat-obsessed kid to draw a floorplan of her dream apartment: a bathroom, a drink vending machine (free with admission), a snack table, video games, and about ten cats and their attendant toys, scratching posts, beds, and climbing structures. Oh, and the furniture is in the beanbag chic style.

Considering all the attention they get, the cats were amazingly friendly, and I'd never seen such a variety of cat breeds up close. (Nor had I ever spent more than ten seconds thinking about cat breeds.) My favorite was a light gray cat with soft fur, which curled up and slept near me while I sat on a beanbag and read a book. Iris made the rounds, drinking a bottomless cup of the vitamin-fortified soda C.C. Lemon and making sure to give equal time to each cat, including the flat-faced feline that looked like it had been beaned with a skillet in old-timey cartoon fashion.

When it was time to pay, we brought out 2000 yen in 10-yen coins. "*Subarashii!*" said the woman working the desk. *Excellent!* I apologized for the unorthodox payment method and offered to count the money myself, but she assured me that wasn't necessary and she would count it later. By the time we got our shoes on, however, she'd already counted out two hundred coins and returned our plastic container.

By the end of our third visit to Nekorobi, I started to get used to having a cat nudge me possessively with the top of its head when I tried to read a book. But I've already made the mistake of admitting in print that we might let Iris get a cat someday, so I'm not going to do *that* again.

Every day when we walked under the green gateway marking the entrance to Pretty Good #1 Alley, an electric eye detected our approach, and a sliding glass door opened and released a cloud of cigarette smoke, the sound of millions of tortured souls crying out from the depths of hell, and a less infernal blast of chilled air. It was the Kokusai Center pachinko parlor.

"You should go in there," said Iris.

"Forget it," I said. "I don't know how to play, and if it's this loud on the street, imagine how loud it is in there."

"But you have to *try* it."

Pachinko is Japan's favorite form of gambling, a vertical pinball machine augmented in recent decades with colorful computer screens and sound effects. The video game Peggle is loosely based on pachinko, in that you launch a ball and then wait to see what happens; there are no flippers. (Please, do not send me emails about how you can earn flippers in Peggle.) In pachinko, the player shoots steel balls into the play area and, depending on where they land, receives more steel balls as a prize.

I know this because when I was a kid, I had my own pachinko machine. It was a fully manual model with a satisfying spring-loaded lever to launch the balls. Looking at photos of classic pachinko machines online, I think mine was quite authentic. Once the ball is launched, it plinks down into a forest of metal pegs and settles into an array of holes that determine your prize. I spent hours playing this thing, because my parents wouldn't buy me an Atari 2600.

Gambling for money in Japan is illegal. Pachinko addicts, however, are not kittens obsessed with shiny objects. Here, as I understand it, is how the money part works: when you win a sackful of silver balls, you can exchange them for a variety of carnival prizes, like at Chuck E. Cheese's. Next door to the pachinko parlor is a pawnshop that will buy your dumb stuffed animals for cash. The pachinko employees aren't supposed to direct anyone to the pawnshop, but if I know the drill, everyone does.

"When are you going to that pachinko parlor, Dada?"

asked Iris.

"If you're so curious, why don't you go in there?"

"I don't think they allow kids. Besides, it would be a good story for your book."

Just down the block from the pachinko parlor was a fugu restaurant, serving raw and cooked blowfish meat. Every time I suggested we try it, Iris said, "NO! You are NOT eating fugu!" Improperly prepared fugu is fatally poisonous. The only people who actually die of fugu poisoning are adrenaline junkies who can't resist just one little taste of the toxic liver, not restaurant patrons. Meanwhile, she couldn't wait to send me into the pachinko parlor to lose all our money.

Eventually, Iris wore me down. She demanded my wallet, then waited outside while I walked into Kokusai Center carrying only a 1000 yen bill, about $10.

Here are a few places quieter than the interior of the Kokusai Center:

- A firing range catering to AK-47 enthusiasts.
- A fire station responding to a massive call, with sirens blaring and engines about to pull out of the garage.
- A metal cast parts factory in full production. (I can vouch for this one, because my father used to work at a cast parts company.)
- An overenrolled preschool after skipping naptime.
- Krakatoa during the 1883 eruption.

But I looked around at the old smoking guys playing pachinko and figured, hey, if these guys aren't deaf, I can hang out here for a few minutes. In retrospect, those guys are unquestionably deaf.

I sat down at one of Kokusai's several hundred pachinko machines and slipped my bill into the slot. Nothing happened. An attendant came over, gave me an unmistakable "you don't belong here" look, and pushed a button to release a few dozen metal balls into an internal tray. Modern pachinko machines don't have a spring-loaded lever like my childhood game; they have a motorized cannon capable of firing several balls per second. All of the strategy is in aiming your balls with tiny degrees of precision.

Even though I used to own a pachinko machine and am a certified Peggle Grand Master (and have been trying for years to figure out a way to brag about this in print), I lost all my money in five minutes. Thank God. At one point, I believe I won a few balls and immediately recycled them back into the machine, but who knows?

"So, how was it?" asked Iris.

"What? Speak up!" I replied.

Ramen

ラーメン

ON OUR FIRST EVENING IN Tokyo, after a ten-hour flight and shuttling efficiently through customs, we took our seats on the Keisei Skyliner, a high-speed train serving Narita Airport. A man asked to see our tickets. He wasn't a conductor; we'd unknowingly sat down in his reserved seat. After finding our actual seats, I went to the vending machine and bought a bottle of C.C. Lemon to share with Laurie and Iris. We drank the fizzy stuff, turned to the window, and watched the city draw us in.

By the time we checked in at our hotel, it was about 6:30 p.m. Tokyo time. That's 2:30 a.m. Seattle time, and it felt like it. The rule for avoiding jet lag (eat and sleep on the local schedule immediately) clashed with the rule for sleepy children (let them stay up a minute too long, and you will be very, very sorry). Hunger lured us out into the streets of Asakusa to look for dinner. We wanted something quick, filling, and cheap. Ramen was preordained. To start, however, we'd have to contend with our first ramen ticket machine.

A ramen ticket machine is an aptitude test, menu, and robot in one box. It stands outside (or just inside) the entrance to a ramen restaurant and has a push button for each menu item: ramen, gyōza, side of rice, and so on. Ticket machines are common at ramen places and rare at other types of restaurants. Some ticket machines have color photos on the buttons, and some have only Japanese writing. If you find yourself in line for a ticket machine that looks problematic, you can order by price and position—the button near the top denoting something that costs between 700 yen and 1000 yen will probably get you a basic bowl of ramen, or you can hit the same button as the person in front of you.

This machine, on Kaminarimon-dōri, had photos. I recognized *tonkotsu* (pork broth) ramen and gyōza. (Ton*kotsu* is different from ton*katsu,* although the "ton" in each refers to pork.) We fed some bills into the machine, received our tickets, and presented them to a waiter. Why do the ticket machines exist? To save the waitstaff from having to stand at your table while you say, "Hmm, maybe I'll have the—no, wait, make that...." Why do they exist only at ramen joints? I don't know.

In Tokyo, ramen is a playground for the culinary imagination. As long as the dish contains thin wheat noodles, it's ramen. In fact, there's a literal ramen playground called Tokyo Ramen Street in the basement of Tokyo Station, with eight top-rated ramen shops sharing one corridor. We stopped by one evening after a day of riding around on the Shinkansen. After drooling over the photos at establishments such as Junk Garage, which serves oily, brothless noodles hidden under a towering slag heap of toppings, we settled on Ramen Honda based on its short line and the fact that its ramen seemed to be topped with a massive pile of scallions. However, anything in Tokyo that appears to be topped with scallions is actually topped with something much better. You'll meet this delectable doppelgänger soon, and in mass quantities.

The Internet is littered with dozens if not hundreds of exclamation point–bedecked ramen blogs (Rameniac, GO RAMEN!, Ramen Adventures, Ramenate!) in English, Japanese, and probably Serbian, Hindi, and Xhosa. In Tokyo, you'll find hot and cold ramen; Thai green curry ramen; diet ramen and ramen with pork broth so thick you could sculpt with it; Italian-inspired tomato ramen; and Hokkaido-style miso ramen. You'll find ramen chains and fiercely individual holes-in-the-wall. Right now, somewhere in the world, someone is having a meet-cute with her first bowl of ramen. As she fills up on pork and noodles and seaweed and bamboo shoots, she thinks, *we were meant to be together,* and she is embarrassed at her atavistic reaction to a simple bowl of soup.

On that first night, as soon as our ramen hit the table, we dove in, parceling out noodles, ultratender braised pork belly, and broth. I ate in a sleepy haze, peering through the glass door of the restaurant. *That's Tokyo out there,* I thought, and grinned. Anyone looking in would have recognized me as a jetlagged sentimental dipshit who just survived his first ramen ticket machine.

In summer, most ramen restaurants in Tokyo serve *hiyashi chūka*, a cold ramen noodle salad topped with strips of ham, cucumber, and omelet; a tart sesame- or soy-based sauce; and sometimes other vegetables, like a tomato wedge or sheets of *wakame* seaweed. The vegetables are arranged in piles of parallel shreds radiating from the center to the edge of the plate like bicycle spokes, and you toss everything together before eating. It's bracing, ice-cold, addictive—summer food from the days before air conditioning.

In Oishinbo: Ramen and Gyōza, a young lifestyle reporter wants to write an article about hiyashi chūka. "I'm not interested in something like hiyashi chūka," says my alter ego Yamaoka. It's a fake Chinese dish made with cheap industrial ingredients, he explains.

Later, however, Yamaoka relents. "Cold noodles, cold soup, and cold toppings," he muses. "The idea of trying to make a good dish out of them is a valid one." Good point, jerk. He mills organic wheat into flour and hires a Chinese chef to make the noodles. He buys a farmyard chicken from an old woman to make the stock and seasons it with the finest Japanese vinegar, soy sauce, and sake. Yamaoka's mean old dad Kaibara Yūzan inevitably gets involved and makes an even better hiyashi chūka by substituting the finest *Chinese* vinegar, soy sauce, and rice wine.

When I first read this, I enjoyed trying to follow the heated argument over this dish I'd never even heard of. Yamaoka and Kaibara are in total agreement that hiyashi chūka needs to be made with quality ingredients, but they disagree about what kind of dish it is: Chinese, Japanese, or somewhere in between? Unlike American food, Japanese cuisine has boundary issues.

For enlightenment, or at least sustenance, I went to Sapporo-ya, a lunch counter in Nihonbashi. According to Yukari Sakamoto, author of the guidebook *Food Sake Tokyo*, Sapporo-ya serves the best hiyashi chūka in town. (Yamaoka gets kicked out of a similar place in Ginza for loudly criticizing the food.) It was a perfect day for cold noodles, cold soup, and cold toppings: during the three-block walk from the subway station to the restaurant, I had to stop at a vending machine for water and then lean against a building, trying not to faint. You know how the weather report sometimes says, "75 degrees (feels like 78)"? In Tokyo in the summer, it's 88 degrees (feels like 375).

Finally, I descended into the basement-level restaurant. In lieu of a ticket machine, a man sits at a podium, takes your order and your cash, and issues a handwritten ticket which you then present to a waitress about six feet away. This did not strike me as particularly efficient, but I wasn't thinking about labor productivity. I was thinking, *This is possibly the ugliest restaurant in the world.*

There are so many thousands of ramen places in Tokyo that it's foolish to generalize about their aesthetic, but many of them make your average hole-in-the-wall ethnic restaurant look like the Four Seasons. They are not actually dirty, because nothing in Tokyo is actually dirty, but they manage to suggest decades of accumulated filth without the filth. The prevailing decor is "if you want decor, go to a fucking *kaiseki* place." Also, many great ramen places smell like pork bones that have been boiling for three days, and when you sit down at the counter, you're inches away from a giant vat of pork bones that have been boiling for three days. Some cooking smells (grilling meat, frying onions) reach into an ancient brain lobe designed to identify good eating; this is not one of them.

The reason for this uncharacteristic inattention to detail is that the ramen shop wants you to understand that they are putting all of their money and energy into the bowl. You'll get a potentially life-changing soup for less than $10. In exchange, you're expected to ignore or learn to appreciate scruffiness. The message: "Our ramen is so good, we don't need to wash our curtain."

You're also supposed to eat fast and get out. A ramen joint is not the place to play Lady and the Tramp with your lover; it's solitary food. One chain, Ichiran, segregates diners into individual booths. You slide into a booth smaller than a study carrel and present your ticket; a faceless server on the other side hands you the soup through a curtain. Nevertheless, Laurie and Iris and I went out for ramen together often, ate slowly by local standards, and always felt welcome—though we never went to Ichiran.

Now, back to Sapporo-ya. The place is deep enough below street level that the windows let in no natural light; harsh fluorescent lamps made everyone look ill. The walls are greenish-yellow. If you are directing a modern adaptation of *The Divine Comedy*, shoot the purgatory scenes here.

The waitress set down my hiyashi chūka *goma dare* (sesame sauce). It was in every way the opposite of its surroundings: colorful, artfully presented, sweated over. The tangle of yellow noodles was served in a shallow blue-and-white bowl and topped with daikon, pickled ginger, roast pork, bamboo shoots, tomato, shredded nori, cucumber, bean sprouts, half a hard-boiled egg, and Japanese mustard. It was almost too pretty to ruin by tossing it together with chopsticks.

I sat at a communal table with two other men. One was a harried-looking businessman in the official summer attire of black pants and a white shirt. He dispatched his hiyashi chūka in five minutes with no apparent shirt stains and went back to work. People in Tokyo are capable of eating noodles at shocking speeds; I lost count of how many times people eating next to me disappeared so quickly that they might as well have left behind a cloud of smoke and a cartoon ZOING! sound. Also at my table, however, was an older man in casual dress, probably retired, who ate nearly as slowly as I did and with evident pleasure. Every bite of hiyashi chūka is a little different but always brought together by the lip-smacking, tangy sauce. As with any bowl of ramen, it is totally appropriate to lift the dish to your mouth and drink the broth, and I did, until it was gone. Yamaoka would not have been impressed—for about $11, there's no way they're using organic or otherwise rarefied ingredients. But it worked for me.

Then I looked around at the horrifying decor and got the hell out of there before I turned out to be the protagonist in a dystopian novel.

Our neighborhood ramen place was called Aoba. That's a joke. There were actually more than fifty ramen places within walking distance of our apartment. But this one was our favorite.

Aoba makes a wonderful and unusual ramen with a mixture of pork and fish broth. The noodles are firm and chewy, and the pork tender and almost smoky, like ham. I also liked how they gave us a small bowl for sharing with Iris without our even asking.

What I really appreciated about this place, however, were two aspects of ramen that I haven't mentioned yet: the eggs and the dipping noodles. After these two, I will stop, but there's so much more to ramen. Would someone please write an English-language book about ramen? Real ramen, not how to cook with Top Ramen noodles? Thanks. (I did find a Japanese-language book called *State-of-the-Art Technology of Pork Bone Ramen* on Amazon. Wish-listed!)

One of the most popular ramen toppings is a soft-boiled egg. Long before sous vide cookery, ramen cooks were slow-cooking eggs to a precise doneness. Eggs for ramen (*ajitsuke tamago*) are generally marinated in a soy sauce mixture after cooking so the whites turn a little brown and the eggs turn a little sweet and salty. I like it best when an egg is plunked whole into the broth so I can bisect it with my chopsticks and reveal the intensely orange, barely runny yolk. A cool egg moistened with rich broth is alchemy. Forget the noodles; I want a ramen egg with a little broth for breakfast.

Finding hot and cold in the same mouthful is another hallmark of Japanese summer food, and many ramen restaurants, including Aoba, feature it in the form of *tsukemen*, dipping noodles. Tsukemen is deconstructed ramen, a bowl of cold cooked noodles and a smaller bowl of hot, ultra-rich broth and toppings. The goal is to lift a tangle of noodles with your chopsticks and dip them in the bowl of broth on the way to your mouth. This is a crazy way to eat noodles and, unless you've been inculcated with the principles of noodle-slurping physics from birth, a great way to ruin your clothes.

The World's Greatest Supermarket

スーパー

No one postures in a supermarket. It's an unfiltered view under those bright lights. You're going to see the real culture and the real cravings and appetites of the people.
—Peter Jon Lindberg

A WHILE BACK, I WAS listening to *The Splendid Table,* and Lynne Rossetto Kasper was talking to Lindberg, a *Travel and Leisure* columnist. The subject? Supermarkets around the world.

"What country do you think has the best supermarkets?" asked Kasper.

Lindberg didn't hesitate. "It has to be Japan," he replied.

The moment I stepped into Life Supermarket in Nakano, I knew what he meant. The name is written in English and pronounced "rye-fuh," and it looks like a small suburban American supermarket, except the only parking lot is for bicycles. Dozens and dozens of bicycles. Bicycle parking lots in Japan can be enormous. Think it's hard to find your car at the airport? I saw a parking lot outside a mall in Asakusa with room for at least a thousand bikes, all spooned together, with none of those helpful cartoon reminders that you're parked in 2C.

Go through the sliding doors and take the escalator down to the basement. If it's a hot day—and in July, it's always a hot day—you'll drink in a welcome blast of air conditioning and, perhaps, a less-welcome blast of the Life Supermarket theme song. This five-second jingle is played on a continuous loop in random parts of the store at random times of day, at various tempos. The song consists of a girlish voice singing, "FUNNY FUNNY FUNNY / SURPRISE, SURPRISE!" over and over and over again.

This induces the Five Stages of Dealing with an Intolerable Jingle. First you laugh. Then you get confused. Then you get angry. Then you go into a wide-eyed trance. Then you load up your basket with Japanese candy bars. In a couple of days, I went from, "Why are they polluting this beautiful supermarket with this terrible song?" to "I don't hear anything, but for some reason, I feel like if I shop here more often I'll get a funny surprise."

This may be a silly thing to say, but Life Supermarket is thoroughly devoted to Japanese food. It's easy to cook Japanese in a small kitchen, and it's just as easy to stock a satisfying range of Japanese ingredients and prepared foods in a small supermarket. Life Supermarket is tiny compared to a suburban American store.

True, there's an aisle devoted to foreign foods, and then there are familiar foods that have been put through the Japanese filter and emerged a little bit mutated. Take breakfast cereal. You'll find familiar American brands such as Kellogg's, but often without English words anywhere on the box. One of the most popular Kellogg's cereals in Japan is Brown Rice Flakes. They're quite good, and the back-of-the-box recipes include cold tofu salad and the savory pancake *okonomiyaki*, each topped with a flurry of crispy rice flakes. Iris and I got mildly addicted to a Japanese brand of dark chocolate cornflakes, the only chocolate cereal I've ever eaten that actually tastes like chocolate. (Believe me, I've tried them all.)

Stocking my pantry at Life Supermarket was fantastically simple and inexpensive. I bought soy sauce, mirin, rice vinegar, rice, salt, and sugar. (I was standing right in front of the salt when I asked where to find it. This happens to me every time I ask for help finding any item in any store.) Total outlay: about $15, and most of that was for the rice. Japan is an unabashed rice protectionist, levying prohibitive tariffs on imported rice. As a result, supermarket rice is domestic, high quality, and very expensive. There were many brands of white rice to choose from, the sacks advertising different growing regions and rice varieties. (I did the restaurant wine list thing and chose the second least expensive.) Japanese consumers love to hear about the regional origins of their foods. I almost never saw ingredients advertised as coming from a particular farm, like you'd see in a farm-to-table restaurant in the U.S., but if the milk is from Hokkaido, the rice from Niigata, and the tea from Uji, all is well. I suppose this is not so different from Idaho potatoes and Florida orange juice.

When I got home, I opened the salt and sugar and spooned some into small bowls near the stove. The next day I learned that Japanese salt and sugar are hygroscopic: their crystalline structure draws in water from the air (and Tokyo, in summer, has enough water in the air to supply the world's car washes). I figured this was harmless and went on licking slightly moist salt and sugar off my fingers every time I cooked.

I went to Life Supermarket as often as possible. It just made me happy. In the produce section, I bought cucumbers, baby bok choy, and ginger, and I was able to choose from stem ginger and young ginger as well as the mature ginger sold in Western markets.

And I bought dozens of *negi*. Negi are sometimes called Japanese leeks or Welsh onions, and in Japan they're often called "Tokyo negi," because they are Tokyo's favorite aromatic vegetable. They're also my favorite. Fatter than scallions but thinner than green onions, negi improve everything. They're sliced thin and used as a garnish on noodles, rice bowls, and tofu; sliced thick, they're found in hot pots and on yakitori skewers. It's like a negi fairy has gone around Tokyo flinging them everywhere. At udon chains, you can buy a cup of extra sliced negi to mound atop your noodles and be your own negi fairy. When we returned to Seattle, going back to food not covered in negi was no fun.

The produce in Japan is eerily perfect and tastes as good as it looks. (Organic produce, however, is rare.) I went around leering at eggplants and squash. I wanted to buy more vegetables than I could cook, just to have them around, much as Senator Phil Gramm once said, "I have more shotguns than I need, but not as many as I want."

Vegetables in Japan are cheap, plentiful, unblemished, and delicious; vegetables five minutes past their prime are taken out back and shot. A supermarket cucumber is one of the greatest pleasures Life Supermarket (and life itself) can offer. Fruit, however, is mostly imported, expensive, and merely OK. We ate a few apples and grapefruits and blueberries that weren't as good as what we get in Seattle. They did have some of those expensive gift melons every visitor to Japan is required to gawk at; because Life is not a fancy store, however, the melons there were only $40, not $100-plus. I started to devise a melon arbitrage scheme involving stuffing my carry-on with Seattle farmers market melons and...okay, I just wanted to say "melon arbitrage."

Next to the fresh produce is the pickle section, a rainbow coalition of preserved vegetables in plastic tubs. The spicier varieties kept luring me in, especially pickled radish stems, cut crosswise into short lengths, salted, and tossed with dried chile. They're a little crunchy and offer a bracing hit of acidity along with a tag-team punch of spice from the radish itself and the red chile. I also enjoyed the spicy vegetable medley with chunks of cucumber, carrot, and napa cabbage. That said, almost nothing I ate in Japan was really that spicy, aside from a Dangerously Spicy Kimchi Rice Ball I bought at a convenience store. Then again, I didn't try about eighty-seven other pickle varieties for sale at Life.

Buying fish in the supermarket in Japan is a delight, even

if the fish is displayed in styrofoam trays, as it is at Life. The most common supermarket fish, mackerel, also happens to be my favorite, and it's sold in a variety of precise quantities. Want three small mackerel fillets? Sure thing. One large? Right over here. Mackerel costs practically nothing and is a snap to cook with the fish grill. I also tried marinated *aji* (Spanish mackerel) but skipped the salmon.

In the freezer case I found a brand of Korean rice dishes that I liked, and potstickers appeared in many guises: raw, cooked, fresh, frozen. My favorite freezer item, however, was frozen water. This is verging on the level of delusion that causes people to ascribe the quality of New York bagels to the local tap water, I know, but Tokyo has really wonderful ice. Sold in resealable plastic bags imprinted with the Japanese character for ice (氷), each clear, slow-melting shard is a unique and ephemeral objet d'art. Every time I came home from Life or anywhere else, I'd artlessly fling off my shoes, plunk a few lovely ice cubes into a glass, and fill it with *mugicha,* or barley tea, which is not really tea, just toasted barley steeped in cold water. You can brew mugicha yourself from loose barley or teabags, but we bought it in large plastic bottles at Life. It tastes ever so slightly like coffee and is said to be especially restorative on a hot day, and in summer in Tokyo there is no other kind of day. I found mugicha perplexing at first and then proceeded to drink gallons of it. The amount of mugicha Tokyo drinks on a July day would fill many swimming pools with uninviting toasty-brown liquid.

The meat section is mostly devoted to presliced meats for hot pots and quick-cooked dishes, with a thin steak or chop here and there. In addition to commodity meat, you'll find Wagyu beef and kurobuta pork. The quality of the meat in an average Tokyo supermarket is higher than at most specialty butchers in the U.S.

Time to fess up. Life Supermarket is not the best supermarket in the world; *every* supermarket in Tokyo is the best supermarket in the world. I haven't even gotten to the prepared food (two different yakitori sections, reheatable fried foods that stay crunchy, and lots of appealing salads and cooked vegetables).

The main floor of Life sells housewares and school supplies. I like these fancy mechanical pencils that are exorbitantly priced and hard to find in Seattle; Life sells them for $5. (I told my friend Emi how pleased I was to find my favorite Uni-Ball pencils there, but I pronounced it "OO-nee ball," which sent her into hysterics. I'd unwittingly said "sea urchin ball.")

The cashiers at Life operate hefty automated cash registers. If you pay with paper money, the cashier inserts the bill into a vertical slot, and any bills in change come out an adjacent slot. The bills are hot to the touch when they emerge from the register, which is oddly satisfying, like it's fresh-baked cash.

To better understand what makes Japan one of the world's greatest places to eat, we should go to 7-Eleven.

7-Eleven is owned by a Japanese company, which is why you sometimes see Hi-Chew for sale at American locations. Tokyo boasts more 7-Elevens (over 1700) than any other city in the world. I realize this sounds like bragging about owning the world's largest collection of dust bunnies, but only if you haven't been to a Tokyo 7-Eleven.

On the last day of our first trip to Tokyo, Iris and I wandered around Asakusa, up the gaudy souvenir arcade of Nakamise-dori, darting in and out of the tiny side streets that feed into it like capillaries. At some point we ended up with our faces pressed against a plate glass window watching an old man make soba. He rolled out the buckwheat noodle dough on a floured table, folded it, and sliced it into noodles with a knife hooked up to a manual rig that supported the weight of the knife while leaving the precision slicing work to the chef. I suggested to Iris that we stop in for a lunch of *zaru soba,* cold buckwheat noodles served in a wicker box. Yes, it looks like you dropped your lunch in a Pier One Imports.

Iris, who inherited my obsessive punctuality and crippling fear of missing a bus, train, or plane, said no, we should stop at 7-Eleven for a bento box and eat it while waiting for the airport train.

Right now I'm sitting three blocks from an American 7-Eleven, so for journalistic accuracy I stopped in to see what I could turn up in the way of a hot, nourishing lunch for under $5. Answer: two taquitos, a Buffalo Chicken Roller, and a Slurpee. Other options included microwaveable beef-and-bean burritos and Lunchable-type deli packs. The lunch philosophy at an American 7-Eleven is *We'll serve whatever can be compressed into a cylinder and displayed near the cash register on the hot dog warmer.* The taquitos were bad in a satisfying junk-foody way. The Buffalo Chicken Roller was just plain bad, a tube of compressed chicken coated with lurid red

Buffalo seasoning powder.

Meanwhile, at a Tokyo 7-Eleven, someone right now is choosing from a variety of bento boxes, delivered that morning and featuring vegetarian sushi, pickled vegetables, tonkatsu. Choose a bento and take it to the counter, and they'll fill it with hot rice, fresh from the rice cooker. Good rice. (To a rounding error, all the rice in Japan is good.) The lunch philosophy at Japanese 7-Eleven? *Actual food.*

On the day we missed out on fresh soba, Iris had a tonkatsu bento, and I chose a couple of rice balls (*onigiri*), one filled with pickled plum and the other with spicy fish roe. For $1.50, convenience store onigiri encapsulate everything that is great about Japanese food and packaging. Let's start in the middle and work outward, like we're building an onion. The core of an onigiri features a flavorful and usually salty filling. This could be an *umeboshi* (pickled apricot, but usually translated as pickled plum), as sour as a Sour Patch Kid; flaked salmon; or cod or mullet roe.

Next is the rice, packed lightly by machine into a perfect triangle. Japanese rice is unusual among staple rices in Asia because it's good at room temperature or a little colder. Sushi or onigiri made with long-grain rice would be a chalky, crumbly disaster. Oishinbo argues that Japan is the only country in Asia that makes rice balls because of the unique properties of Japanese rice. I doubt this. Medium- and short-grain rices are also popular in parts of southern China, and presumably wherever those rices exist, people squish them into a ball to eat later, kind of like I used to do with a fistful of crustless white bread. (Come on, I can't be the only one.)

Next comes a layer of cellophane, followed by a layer of nori and another layer of cellophane. The nori is preserved in a transparent shell for the same reason Han Solo was encased in carbonite: to ensure that he would remain crispy until just before eating. (At least, I assume that's what Jabba the Hutt had in mind.) You pull a red strip on the onigiri packaging, both layers of cellophane part, and a ready-to-eat rice ball tumbles into your hand, encased in crispy seaweed.

Not everybody finds the convenience store onigiri packaging to be a triumph. "The seaweed isn't just supposed to be crunchy," says Futaki in Oishinbo: The Joy of Rice. "It tastes best when the seaweed gets moist and comes together as one with the rice." Yamaoka agrees. Jerk.

Once we were living in Nakano, not a day went by without a trip to a *kombini*, which is Japanese for "convenience store." Not just 7-Eleven, but also FamilyMart, Lawson, Mini Stop, and Daily Yamazaki. Iris kept referring to the last as "Dried-out Yamaoka," which never got less funny.

There is no secret to what makes kombini so great. The stores look just like American convenience stores inside and out, but the products for sale reflect a national obsession with quality. Mostly I'm talking about food, but at one point I bought a $1 Campus-brand notebook at 7-Eleven, and it has proven durable and well-designed, probably my favorite notebook. Another popular brand of notebook in Japan is named for the phrase "living art" in French: VIFART. If you think this is funny, you are my kind of person.

The hot case at a kombini features tonkatsu, fried chicken, *menchikatsu* (a breaded hamburger patty), Chinese pork buns, potato croquettes, and seafood items such as breaded squid legs or oysters. In a bit of international solidarity, you'll see corn dogs, often labeled "Amerikandoggu."

One day for lunch I stopped at 7-Eleven and brought home a pouch of "Gold Label" beef curry, steamed rice, *inarizushi* (sushi rice in a pouch of sweetened fried tofu), cold noodle salad, and a banana. Putting together lunch for the whole family from an American 7-Eleven would be as appetizing as scavenging among seaside medical waste, but this was fun to shop for and fun to eat.

Instant ramen is as popular in Japan as it is in college dorms worldwide, and while the selection of flavors is wider than at an American grocery, it serves a predictable ecological niche as the food of last resort for those with no money or no time. (Frozen ramen, on the other hand, can be very good; if you have access to a Japanese supermarket, look for Myojo Chukazanmai brand.) That's how I saw it, at least, until stumbling on the ramen topping section in the 7-Eleven refrigerator case, where you can buy shrink-wrapped packets of popular fresh ramen toppings such as braised pork belly and fermented bamboo shoots. With a quick stop at a convenience store, you can turn instant ramen into a serious meal. The pork belly is rolled and tied, braised, chilled, and then sliced into thick circular slices like Italian pancetta. This is one of the best things you can do with pork, and I don't say that lightly.

Every kombini, just like an American convenience store, has a section of salty beer snacks. Here, though, they're worth eating with or without beer. We got hooked on a cracker called

Cheeza, which looks like a small wedge of Swiss cheese, complete with holes. Cheeza comes in various flavors, and the package is labeled with the percentage of cheese found in the product, like the cocoa percentage on a fancy chocolate bar. The least-cheesy Cheeza is over 50 percent cheese and has a great sturdy crunch. If you've spent decades eating American candy and snacks, in Japan you will constantly be saying, "Hey, this really tastes like...!" Another tasty cheese-based snack consists of dried cubes of pure cheese with toasted almonds. The beer snacks section also offers lots of fish-based snacks: tiny dried anchovies with slivered almonds, dried squid, and other things with tentacles.

Occasionally, I'd stop and browse the magazine section, especially food magazines like Orange Page, Today's Food, and a men's cooking magazine with lots of meat recipes. Japanese-language food magazines are so well illustrated that you could make a good stab at cooking the recipes without being able to read a word of Japanese.

There *is* one thing wrong with Tokyo 7-Eleven: no Slurpees.

For outrageous high-end food shopping, the opposite of a kombini, the place to go is a *depachika,* the basement food section of a department store. Tokyo has dozens of large department stores, and every one has a depachika.

A depachika is like nothing else. It is the endless bounty of a hawker's bazaar, but with Japanese civility. It is Japanese food and foreign food, sweet and savory. The best depachika have more than a hundred specialized stands and cannot be understood on a single visit. I felt as though I had a handle on

Life Supermarket the first time I shopped there, but I never felt entirely comfortable in a depachika. They are the food equivalent of Borges's "The Library of Babel": if it's edible, someone is probably selling it, but how do you find it? How do you resist the cakes and spices and Chinese delis and bento boxes you'll pass on the way?

At the Isetan depachika, in Shinjuku, French pastry god Pierre Hermé sells his signature cakes and macarons. Not to be outdone, Franco-Japanese pastry god Sadaharu Aoki sells his own nearby. Tokyo is the best place in the world to eat French pastry. The quality and selection are as good as or better than in Paris, and the snootiness factor is zero.

I wandered by a collection of things on sticks: yakitori at one stand, *kushiage* at another. Kushiage are panko-breaded and fried foods on sticks. At any depachika, you can buy kushiage either golden and cooked, or pale and raw to fry at home. Neither option is terribly appetizing: the fried stuff is losing crispness by the second, and who wants to deep-fry in a poorly ventilated Tokyo apartment in the summer? But the overall effect of the display is mesmerizing: look at all the different foods they've put on sticks! Pork, peppers, mushrooms, squash, taro, and two dozen other little cubes.

At Isetan I found a stand selling little Chinese spring rolls in a variety of flavors, and nothing else. Another stand, at another depachika, sold only *nikuman,* the Japanese version of those fluffy steamed Chinese pork buns. I lost track of how many depachika I visited, but every time, especially at Takashimaya department store in Nihonbashi, I found myself staring down the pickle section.

The pickle (*tsukemono*) section at a depachika is like a scene from a fresh vegetable market in Latin America that has been attacked by Bunnicula. While the pickles at Life Supermarket are secreted away in retortable tubs and blister packs and shrink-wrap, here in the Takashimaya basement they come out for sunbathing and free sampling: fragrant (OK, stinky) rice-bran *nukazuke,* amber sake-lees *Narazuke,* tiny blue pickled eggplants, red pickled ginger, pink pickled ginger, cucumbers pickled in the briny byproduct of producing umeboshi, salty pickled apricots. The umeboshi themselves, in at least half a dozen varieties, are found at a nearby stand. Desiccated daikon stretch across the counter like sleeping snakes.

If all of this sounds unfamiliar, most of it was unfamiliar to me, too, even after copious free sampling and dozens of meals with little piles of pickles served alongside. Japan has the second most sophisticated pickling culture in the world (after Korea), and many of its vegetables are pickled into submission, pickled until they look nothing like the vine-ripened point of origin. Even after I took a pickle class from Tokyo-based cookbook author Elizabeth Andoh, the pickle counter remained for me a confounding microcosm of the depachika, which was in turn a microcosm of the blissfully overwhelming sprawl of Tokyo itself.

Japanese Breakfast

朝ご飯

AT THE RISK OF OFFENDING everyone in every country, I think there are only two great breakfasts in the world.

The first is leftover pizza, reheated as follows. Place the slice, topping-side down, in a nonstick pan over medium heat. When it's sizzling and the cheese and toppings are a little brown and crusty, flip the slice and continue cooking until hot. Trust me. I learned this method from a guy known only as Tommy who was presumably smoking something known as Mary Jane when he invented it.

The second is Japanese breakfast. The key parts of this complete breakfast are rice, pickles, and miso soup, and that trio on its own is a perfectly satisfying breakfast. At a hotel or restaurant, however, you'll always get grilled fish and often a cooked vegetable dish, tofu, and eggs. A full-on Japanese breakfast at a nice hotel or inn often comprises seven or more courses but never feels overwhelming; it is simultaneously lavish and restrained. Unlike the traditional English fry-up, which I also admire, I can devour a Japanese breakfast and feel ready to meet the day, rather than the pillow.

Rice at breakfast is usually served with nori in plastic packets. You unwrap the plastic, place the strip of nori on top of your rice bowl, use your chopsticks to fold it around a ball of rice (like an impromptu mini-onigiri), dip it lightly in soy sauce, and, if you've made it this far, eat it. Wrangling crisp nori into position with chopsticks is beyond Ordinary Wizarding Level skill, and this morning feat of mechanical engineering challenges even locals. In Oishinbo: Japanese Cuisine, Yamaoka castigates his hapless editor, Tomii, for saturating his nori in soy sauce before applying it to his rice: "You shouldn't waste the efforts of the people who work hard to put the nori inside the little wrappers so it stays crisp."

Nori, incidentally, is also part of the traditional breakfast in Wales, where it is made into laverbread, nori paste breaded in oatmeal and fried. Same seaweed, different coast.

Fish at breakfast is sometimes *himono* (semi-dried fish, intensely flavored and chewy, the Japanese equivalent of a breakfast of kippered herring or smoked salmon) and sometimes a small fillet of rich, well-salted broiled fish. Japanese cooks are expert at cutting and preparing fish with nothing but salt and high heat to produce deep flavor and a variety of textures: a little crispy over here, melting and juicy there. Some of this is technique and some is the result of a turbocharged supply chain that scoops small, flavorful fish out of the ocean and deposits them on breakfast tables with only the briefest pause at Tsukiji fish market and a salt cure in the kitchen.

By now, I've finished my fish and am drinking miso soup. Where you find a bowl of rice, *miso shiru* is likely lurking somewhere nearby. It is most often just like the soup you've had at the beginning of a sushi meal in the West, with wakame seaweed and bits of tofu, but Iris and I were always excited when our soup bowls were filled with the shells of tiny *shijimi* clams. Clams and miso are one of those predestined culinary combos—what clams and chorizo are to Spain, clams and miso are to Japan. Shijimi clams are fingernail-sized, and they are eaten for the briny essence they release into the broth, not for what Mario Batali has called "the little bit of snot" in the shell. Miso-clam broth is among the most complex soup bases you'll ever taste, but it comes together in minutes, not the hours of simmering and skimming involved in making European stocks. As Tadashi Ono and Harris Salat explain in their book *Japanese Hot Pots,* this is because so many fermented Japanese ingredients are, in a sense, already "cooked" through beneficial bacterial and fungal actions.

Japanese food has a reputation for crossing the line from subtlety into blandness, but a good miso-clam soup is an umami bomb that begins with dashi made from *kombu* (kelp) and *katsuobushi* (bonito flakes) or *niboshi* (a school of tiny dried sardines), adds rich miso pressed through a strainer for smoothness, and is then enriched with the salty clam essence.

If miso soup is one of the most approachable, familiar, and reassuring breakfast dishes for the Western palate, *nattō* is certainly the least. Like tofu and miso, nattō is a fermented soybean product. The small, whole beans are sold in single-serving styrofoam tubs; it looks innocuous enough when you open the package, but when you stir it up, a viscous, stringy web fights back. The more you stir, the more slimy and obstreperous the mass becomes. To nattō lovers, this is a feature. Once you've coaxed out enough stringy, matted bacterial residue to make you happy, eat the nattō with rice and soy sauce, and maybe even a raw egg for added creaminess.

Nattō remains one of the Japanese staple foods least known in the West. I don't expect this to change in the next few centuries. Did I mention nattō also smells funky? I'm unusual, I think, in finding nattō neither delicious nor terrifying. To me it tastes a little like coffee. I don't actively seek it out, but it doesn't send me into the fetal position like *junsai*, which we'll meet soon.

Eggs appear at breakfast in a variety of forms, often as *tamagoyaki*. You've met this sweetened omelet at your local sushi place, where it's considered beginner sushi. In Tokyo, good tamagoyaki is an object of lust. Cut into thick blocks and served at room temperature, a creamy monolith of tamagoyaki is somehow the antithesis of American breakfast eggs. It can be made at home in a special square or rectangular frying pan, but it's also for sale in supermarkets, at depachika, and at Tsukiji fish market. Most people who aren't sushi chefs buy it. My tamagoyaki-making skills are nonexistent, but I sometimes flavor beaten eggs with soy sauce, dashi, and mirin and make an omelet to eat with rice and nori.

I've enjoyed a full-service Japanese breakfast at a nice little urban hotel but also at Denny's. Tokyo Denny's is a total head trip. It looks like an American Denny's circa 1982, complete with a cigarette machine and plenty of smokers. The menu, however, is written in Japanese and specializes in *yōshoku.*

Yōshoku is the Japanese take on Western foods; much of it was created during the Meiji period (1868–1912), when, after centuries of isolation, Japan began importing goods and ideas from the outside world, including food. Yōshoku dishes such as *hambaagu* (salisbury steak in brown sauce), curry rice, potato croquettes, and "spaghetti *naporitan*" are now much-loved comfort food. They're also so unlike the dishes that inspired them that they tend to be really hard for Westerners to appreciate.

When I asked Tokyoites about their favorite food, the answer was almost always something in the yōshoku canon. My friend Emi, for example, told me her favorite food is *omuraisu,* fried rice wrapped in an omelet and topped with ketchup, a dish found on the kid's menu at Denny's.

At breakfast, however, the menu bifurcates into Japanese and American breakfast. There are no Grand Slams, but the French toast and pancakes aren't bad; Iris is partial to the Koala Pancake, a short stack of pancakes topped with two Cocoa Puff eyes and a vanilla ice cream nose. Many of the Western breakfast dishes come with a green salad. The Japanese breakfast set with fish, rice, nattō, miso soup, and pickles is quite good and priced well under $10. Yoshinoya, the largest beef-bowl chain, also serves a traditional breakfast set and charges even less—about $5. Like Denny's, Yoshinoya is open 24 hours, and in the morning the clientele is old guys drinking coffee or tea. The ambience is more like an American diner than most American diners.

At home, we generally had a Western breakfast: fruit, yogurt, cereal, bacon, toast, and tea. One day we were out of milk, and Laurie ran out early to the Mini Stop convenience store for a pint of milk for her Daily Club black tea, which she found at Life Supermarket. (The tea was shelved in two sections, one for green tea and one for everything else.) She returned with a pint carton, poured some milk into her tea, and did a spit-take. It wasn't milk; it was drinkable Bulgarian-style yogurt. "It says Bulgaria in big letters right on the carton," I pointed out helpfully. Laurie held the carton out toward me and made a face as sour as drinkable yogurt. What it actually said on the carton was: ブルガリア. (Iris and I can read some Japanese. Laurie can't.)

White bread in Japan is a steroidal megaloaf called *shokupan*. Brioche-like and great for toasting, shokupan is sold in bags of four, six, or eight perfectly square slices, without heels. Where do the heels go? Out back with the imperfect vegetables?

I bought shokupan several times before figuring out why the four-, six-, and eight-slice sacks all sold for the same price. It's the same loaf, cut into thicker or thinner slices. Eight-slice shokupan is similar in thickness to Wonder bread. Six-slice shokupan is like what we buy in Seattle as Texas Toast (the fresh kind, not the frozen garlic bread). A piece of four-slice shokupan is like a Stephen King paperback. It would make a slot toaster cry out in pain. Iris and I liked the six-slice bread best and usually ate it toasted with melted butter and a sprinkle of sea salt.

Next time I have breakfast at an American Denny's, there's going to be an international incident. What do you mean you don't serve miso soup and Uji green tea? This is Denny's, isn't it? Fine, I'll just have some coffee and a pack of Marlboros.

Tofu

豆腐

Tofu is having a bit of a moment.

Sure, it's still the butt of hack jokes and the presumed sustenance of sad vegetarians who close their eyes and think of steak. In Japan as in much of Asia, however, people eat tofu because they like it. Iris and I recently had a gaga-for-tofu experience at home in Seattle, and it was all Andrea Nguyen's fault.

Nguyen is the author of three cookbooks, an authority on Vietnamese food, and a person blessed with the ability to land a book smack in the middle of a current food trend. Her book *Asian Tofu* came out in 2012, and if the title sounds a little weird (what is tofu if not Asian?), it's a warning: this book celebrates tofu in its natural habitat and doesn't force it to pose as meat or hide it away in a burrito.

When I received Andrea's book, I flipped right past the

lengthy section on how to make homemade tofu, because I was, like, *please*. Seattle has no shortage of tofu. Even the stuff at Trader Joe's is pretty good. Then I started reading about tofu skins.

If you already hate tofu, the term "tofu skin" is probably an effective emetic. But this stuff is addictive. You start by making fresh soy milk. I'm not going to soft-pedal how much work this is: you have to soak, grind, squeeze, and simmer dried soybeans. The result is a thick milk entirely unlike the soy milk you get in a box at Whole Foods in the same way Parmigiano-Reggiano is unlike Velveeta.

Then, to make tofu skins (*yuba* in Japanese), you simmer the soy milk gently over low heat until a skin forms on the surface, then pluck it off with your fingers and drape it over a chopstick to dry. It is exactly like the skin that forms on top of pudding, the one George Costanza wanted to market as Pudding Skin Singles. Yuba doesn't look like much—like a pile of discarded raw chicken skin, honestly. But the texture is toothsome, and with each bite you're rewarded with the flavor of fresh soy milk. It's best served with just a few drops of soy sauce and maybe some grated ginger or sliced negi.

"I'm kind of obsessed with tofu skins right now," said Iris, poking her head into the fridge to grab a round of yuba. Me too.

In Seattle, I had to buy, grind, boil, and otherwise toil for a few sheets of yuba. In Tokyo, I found it at Life Supermarket, sold in a single-serving plastic tub with a foil top. The yuba wasn't as snappy or flavorful as homemade, but it had that characteristic fresh-soy aroma, which to me smells like a combination of "healthy forest" and "clean baby." Iris and I ate it greedily. (The yuba, not the baby.)

Yuba isn't technically tofu, because the soy milk isn't co-agulated. Japanese tofu comes in two basic categories, much like underpants: cotton (*momen*) and silken (*kinugoshi*). Cotton tofu is the kind eaten most commonly in the U.S.; if you buy a package of extra-firm tofu and cut it up for stir-frying, that's definitely cotton tofu.

Silken tofu is fragile, creamier and more dairy-like than cotton tofu, and it's the star of my favorite summer tofu dish. *Hiya yakko* is cubes of tofu, usually silken, drizzled with soy sauce and judiciously topped with savory bits: grated ginger or daikon, bonito flakes, negi. It's popular in Japanese bars and easy to make at home, which I did, with (you will be shocked to hear) tons of fresh negi.

Western food offers a wide variety of flavors and a limited palette of textures. If you grew up in the West, think about how many of your favorite foods are, as in the famous Far Side cartoon, crunchy on the outside with a chewy center.

This particular textural contrast is certainly prized in Japan—witness the ubiquity of tonkatsu and potato croquettes. But the Asian appreciation for textural variety extends into every corner of the spectrum, including some shady areas most Westerners would rather keep well-shaded. As Fuchsia Dunlop writes in her memoir, *Shark's Fin and Sichuan Pepper*:

> Texture is the last frontier for Westerners learning to appreciate Chinese food. Cross it, and you're really inside.

But the way there is a wild journey that will bring you face to face with your own prejudices, your childhood fears, perhaps even some Freudian paranoias.

The same goes for Japanese food. For example, I went to a street fair at Nakano Sun Plaza and had a free sample of *warabi mochi*. You may be familiar with *mochi*, sometimes called rice taffy, which is cooked sticky rice pounded into a very thick paste. Warabi mochi is not that. It's made from bracken starch and is more bouncy and marshmallowy than rice mochi. If you fell off a ledge and landed in a big vat of warabi mochi, you'd be fine, albeit well-dusted with *kinako* (sweetened soybean powder) or matcha. The matcha-dusted warabi mochi I tasted was delicious, and it was still delicious after I'd been chewing it for a couple of minutes, which is rather a common experience in Japan. On the menu at our favorite yakitori place, they list "tender chicken," just as you'd see in the U.S., but also "chewy chicken." Each is very much as advertised. The chewy chicken is certainly more flavorful. It is also so chewy that I amassed a wad of half-chewed chewy chicken in the corner of my mouth, like that Japanese video game where a sticky ball rolls around gathering debris and mass. Eventually I had to spit it out in the bathroom.

Or consider the Japanese love of things slimy and sticky. One rainy day, we dashed into a soba restaurant for shelter and lunch. When we stepped inside, two women were vigorously grating *nagaimo* for *tororo soba*. Dear Penthouse Forum: I never thought this would happen to me.

Nagaimo, *Dioscorea opposita*, is a mountain tuber that

looks like a daikon that forgot to shave its legs. When you grate it, it turns to a viscous white slime called *tororojiru*. A popular delicacy in Japan is cod or blowfish milt (*shirako*). "Milt" is just a euphemistic word for sperm. But tororojiru, despite hailing from the plant kingdom, is much more se-men-like than shirako. At the table next to us, two women were having lunch, dipping their cold soba into a sauce heavy with tororojiru, and slurping away. I've also seen a noodle dish combining nagaimo slime with natto, raw egg, and whatever other gluey stuff happens to be on hand. People eat this stuff not because they're on *Fear Factor* or because of any nutritional dogma. They simply enjoy it.

I can go part way down this road. For breakfast, I enjoy *on-tama udon*, noodles in a *shōyu*-based sauce topped with a very runny soft-boiled egg. (Shōyu is just the Japanese word for soy sauce, but it has a nice ring, doesn't it?) Honestly, I considered myself pretty texturally adventurous until I met my nemesis in the form of junsai.

It happened at Ukai Tofu-ya, an upscale tofu restaurant in Shiba Park, near Tokyo Tower. First, try to imagine an up-scale tofu restaurant in the U.S., and get all the giggles out of your system. Done? Good. The approach to Ukai is a quintes-sential Tokyo experience: you emerge from the subway onto a baking-hot boulevard, drag yourself across busy streets and blank walls, and then emerge, suddenly, into a garden out of time, overgrown in a deliberate fashion, an oasis that makes the adjacent brutal urbanism invisible. Ukai is a huge restau-rant, but they seat every party out of the line of sight of any other, so for the length of your meal, the place is yours.

If the level of service at a Tokyo doughnut shop is comparable to the best restaurant in most countries, the service at an upscale tofu restaurant is positively disarming. I found myself thanking the waitresses in a girlish whisper for each course: the sashimi, the fried tofu slathered with miso, the perfect little pickles, the single fresh loquat hidden inside a *hōzuki* lantern plant. Then came the cold tofu course. I had come to Ukai to taste the freshest, creamiest tofu Tokyo could serve up, and now it was before me, two lumps of tofu made from Hokkaido soybeans, in a large bowl of kombu dashi with some sort of greens floating in the broth.

I asked about the vegetable. "Junsai," explained the waitress. She transferred the tofu to a smaller bowl, ladled dashi over it, and then went after every last bit of junsai with a miniature swimming pool net. No one, this gesture implied, would want to miss out on one bit of junsai, although it looked more like thorny prunings than anything edible.

Here is the good news: junsai does not have the texture of woody twigs. It is, however, the most mucilaginous food I can possibly imagine. Okra thinks junsai is too slimy. As Wikipedia understates it:

> It is identified by its bright green leaves, small purple flowers that bloom from June through September, and a thick mucilage that covers all of the underwater organs, including the underside of the leaves, stems, and developing buds.

Yes, junsai is certainly distinctive: each tiny leaf and bud is fully encased in a snot bubble. If you make it through that alive, the texture of the twig itself is snappy, easy to chew, not bad at all by comparison.

And I had a lot of junsai to make it through. I started by dispatching the tofu, which was everything I'd hoped for: creamy, light, and redolent of fresh soy milk. It was the best tofu of my life, and I was about to ruin the memory of it by turning to the junsai. It was like capping off a beautiful wedding with a series of chainsaw murders. I grimaced through each morsel of slime. *This is a beautiful restaurant where people come to eat great food,* I thought to myself. *They wouldn't deliberately play a trick on me. People pay good money for a hearty serving of junsai.* These mental gymnastics failed to convince me I was eating anything other than pond snot. At one point I really thought I might throw up and get deported.

Reader, I ate all the junsai. When the waitress came over to take my bowl, I smiled and said, "*Oishikatta.*" Delicious. The quiver in my voice was more defeat than awe.

Junsai is a seasonal delicacy. You know how some people annoy you all year by talking about how excited they are for rhubarb or tomato season? If I lived in Japan, I would spend all summer anticipating the end of junsai season.

Having defeated my viscous nemesis, I sat back in my chair at Ukai and relaxed. Now I could enjoy dessert: slimy *kuzu* starch noodles in sugar syrup with pickled apricots.

If the most common knock on tofu is that it is bland, odd-textured, and incapable of starring in visceral food memories, my lunch proved that false. When I think back on the best meals I ate in Tokyo, that creamy tofu keeps insisting

on its proper place. Anyone could love tofu.
Junsai, maybe not.

Just an American Girl in the Tokyo Streets

子供

IT WAS PROBABLY WHEN IRIS put on her lab coat and prepared to stick a thermometer up a cat's rectum that it struck me just how much responsibility and freedom kids enjoy in Tokyo.

OK, the cat was fake, but the look of concentration on Iris's face was genuine. We were at Kidzania, an international chain of theme parks where children work at realistic fake occupations: veterinarians, airline pilots, firefighters, pizza cooks, building maintenance technicians, and dozens of other jobs.

In its dedication to aping all aspects of an activity down to the least enticing, Kidzania is absurd and delightful, and I'm not just talking about cat rectums. Iris wanted to drive a little car. So she got in line at the Kidzania DMV and waited for a full hour to get her license to drive a car which, if it collided with you at full speed, might cause a minor shin bruise. While Iris enjoyed the faithful simulation of modern bureaucratic hell, she watched the gas station attendants receive their training, which had nothing to do with fire safety or pump operations and every thing to do with bowing in unison after dispensing imaginary gasoline.

Finally street legal, Iris got in her car and pulled up to the gas station. The gas jockey curtain call went off without a hitch. Most of the kids at Kidzania were ages five to ten. We stuck around to watch Iris do her thing. Most parents left their kids in the care of the Kidzania attendants, a college-age bunch whose patience with children would be the envy of pediatricians, Disney employees, and actual parents everywhere. Iris also worked as a produce inspector ("We measured the sweetness of the banana with a refractometer!") and a building maintenance technician, which required her to climb a ladder to the second story of a building, repair a broken window, and rappel down. As a lifelong acrophobe, I would pay theme-park prices not to do this.

A more laid-back children's paradise can be found at the Ghibli (pronounced "jibbly") Museum in suburban Mitaka. Studio Ghibli is the production company founded by Hayao Miyazaki, creator of the animated films *Spirited Away, Ponyo,* and the masterpiece *My Neighbor Totoro.*

The Ghibli Museum was built as a fanciful pastiche of European styles, an architecture seen in many Miyazaki films. It opened in 2001 but feels much older, partly because the build quality and detail is unreal compared to any theme park architecture you've ever seen. Photography is prohibited, and children are encouraged to ditch their parents and explore the place on their own (are you sensing a pattern yet?). Iris spent most of her time climbing on a plush replica of the Cat Bus from *Totoro* and flinging stuffed soot sprites. This will make sense if you've seen the movie, and if you haven't, well, I don't want to be one of those guys who starts sentences with, "You haven't seen...?"

Iris was also obsessed with the Totoro zoetrope. A zoetrope is an optical illusion invented, I think, to torture writers, in that I could go on for six pages trying to describe a zoetrope, and you'd still have no idea what I was talking about. Watch three seconds of a zoetrope video on YouTube, however, and you'll say, "Oh, it's one of those things."

After a couple of hours at both Kidzania and Ghibli, I got restless. This is partly because I have a short attention span; Laurie would have stayed at the Ghibli Museum for days, and I'm pretty sure we could have dropped Iris off at Kidzania and picked her up the following summer as an actual licensed veterinarian. But I was eager to get back to the main attraction. Creating a safe and entertaining theme park where kids can run wild and parent-free is a nice achievement. Creating a city of 35 million where they can do the same is unparalleled in the history of the world.

Tokyo is clean, glistening, and functional. Its parks and playgrounds are the opposite: strewn with cigarette butts and other litter, equipped with rusty eighties play equipment, and chronically underused. There is a park near our apartment, on the way to the laundromat, that consists of a pair of uneven bars, a drinking fountain, and an ashtray on a packed-dirt surface. Adults sometimes use it for morning calisthenics, but not often.

My theory is that Tokyo parks are ugly and neglected because they're unnecessary. In America, adults go to parks to relax in semitranquil surroundings, and children go there to play. In Tokyo, adults relax at shrines and bathhouses. And where do children play? In the street, of course.

Given a street to play in, kids will never choose a park. The park is blocks away, and we want to play *right now.* In most of America, playing in the street is assumed to be suicidal. When I was growing up in Portland, Oregon, in the eighties, we lived on a quiet residential street on the outskirts of town, and my brothers and I played in the street when we could get away with it, but my most vivid memory of street play is my dad getting into a shouting match with a crazy driver who almost plowed into us as he screamed down the street in his Mercedes. We used to say "go play in traffic" to mean "go fuck yourself."

On our street in Nakano, playing in the street is just what kids do. It's assumed to be safe because it is safe. Residential streets in Nakano are narrow and don't have sidewalks. Cars are welcome, and pedestrians and bikes are expected to get out of the way to let them pass, but the cars slink along so slowly, it's as if they're embarrassed.

Immediately after we moved in, Iris met Zen, who lived in our building and who was every inch the word "boy" in human form. Zen was five and spoke no English other than "hello!" and "see you!" Iris spoke very little Japanese. This, of course, didn't interfere with their play at all. Minutes after meeting, they stole tomato stakes from Zen's parents' garden and started fencing. They played tag; they played baseball; they shot each other with plastic or imaginary guns; they sprayed each other with the hose. At any time of day, Zen would appear below our balcony, yelling "IRIS-CHAN!" or ring our doorbell six hundred times. One night, to Iris's delight, he set off a bunch of fireworks in the alley. Naming him "Zen" was presumably wishful thinking.

Summoned by Zen, Iris would run out to play in the street. If Iris didn't feel like playing, Zen would bellow her name for ten minutes before giving up. I'm glad I rarely had to intervene in this relationship, because Zen found my broken Japanese hilarious. Anything I said, he would repeat like it was the funniest thing ever, probably because I said something like, "Iris Zen play very good, yes? But we go dinnering now."

Zen had a little sidekick named Kotaro. I never heard him speak. He always seemed to be standing just behind Zen and to the side, grinning like a maniac. If they were characters in a comic, Zen would be the mouth and Kotaro the muscle. Admittedly, Kotaro weighed about forty pounds, but he had the attitude down. There were also a couple of girls who lived across the street and came out to play sometimes. American parents who bemoan the rise of the play date and the demise of spontaneous play should visit Japan. Many aspects of suburban Tokyo life are ripped from wistful American memoirs and Richard Scarry books. One morning we walked with Zen and his mother to kindergarten, and shopkeepers and people on the street kept hailing us to say good morning. One man leaned out of his store to say, "*Zen, bōshi wa doko desu ka?*" Zen, where's your hat? His mother half-smiled and held up the hat.

Like many people in the neighborhood, Zen's parents are avid vegetable gardeners, and they kept us supplied with homegrown cucumbers. Supermarket cucumbers in Japan are superb; just-picked cucumbers are revelatory. Plus, they come with the free spectacle of opening the door to Zen with a cucumber in each hand, sheepishly offering them forth. Is there any facial expression more universal than *my parents are making me do this embarrassing thing*?

Laurie bought Zen's family a gift to thank them for all the cucumbers: a cucumber-print *tenugui* hand cloth, meticulously gift-wrapped. She gave it to Iris and said, "Would you please take this to Zen and make sure he gives it to his parents?" Iris shrugged at the idea of trying to make Zen do anything, but she took the gift bag and headed downstairs.

About ten minutes later, we came down and followed a trail of torn wrapping paper to find Zen in the street, the cucumber tenugui draped around his neck, totally pimped out, shouting commands to Kotaro and exhorting Iris to blow off dinner and come play instead.

Children in Japan are free to do much more than simply play in the street. You see unaccompanied minors on the train constantly, usually girls in their navy blue school uniforms heading to or from school, or evening cram school, or activities. Not just thirteen-year-olds, but plenty of street-smart eight-year-olds riding and walking fearlessly through the world's busiest train system.

Washington Post reporter T.R. Reid moved with his family to Tokyo in the nineties. Shortly after they arrived, his daughter begged him to let her and her friend, both ten years old, go to Tokyo Disneyland. Sure thing, said Reid, who promptly called the friend's mom and offered to chaperone the outing. "Huh?" said the perplexed mom. He ended up letting the kids go solo, which is what his daughter had been asking for all along. The kids had a great time, certainly more so than if *Dad* had come along.

Parents in Tokyo aren't afraid of crime or car accidents, and they have little reason to be. The largest city in the world is also among the safest. I'm among the least crime-obsessed Americans I know, but in Tokyo even I had to slip into a different mindset. Worrying about being the victim of a crime in Tokyo is a waste of mental energy on par with worrying about being struck by lightning, and slowly you begin to realize how many of our decisions are circumscribed by the probability that someone is going to interfere with us. Wouldn't it be nice to leave our computers unattended at a cafe, carry around plenty of cash, and send our eight-year-olds to pick up a bunch of leeks? (Oddly, bike theft is common in Japan, but nobody uses U-locks.)

The Japanese know that sending their kids out unaccompanied is an exceptional privilege, and they made a popular TV show about it. On *First Errands*, extremely young kids are sent out, under the eye of a camera crew, on implausible errands. A two-year-old girl goes to the supermarket for milk and gyōza sauce. The bag is too heavy for her to carry, so she drags it along the ground, and the milk carton bursts open and starts leaking. (Every episode of *First Errands* features a moment where any parent watching the show will burst into tears.) Sobbing, the girl returns to the store, and the folks at the service desk help her tape up the milk and send her home to her parents.

So we started sending Iris and her coin purse to Life Supermarket. We told her she could stop for water at Vending Machine Corner and buy herself a treat at the store. You've never seen a kid more proud than Iris returning from her first solo visit to Life with a plastic-wrapped tray of fruit. "And I brought back 2 yen in change," she reported. The fruit tray featured an apple, a grapefruit, an orange, a kiwi, and some fake paper leaves. I would never have bought a fruit tray, which is exactly the point. *Dad* wasn't there to say something dumb like, "We can choose our *own* fruit assortment."

We sent Iris to Life a couple of times a week, mostly for vegetables. She often bought herself a package of Hi-Chew or Choco Baby candy. Soon she started arguing that she could easily go to Aigre-Douce, our favorite patisserie, by herself, too. "I know *exactly* how to get there," said Iris. "Chūō Rapid to Shinjuku, change to the Yamanote line, get off at Mejiro, walk down Mejiro-dōri..." And I'm sure she was right, but we were too American to let her try it. Given another couple of months, though, I'm sure we would have relented.

Crush Hour

時間を急ぐ

"THIS ISN'T CRUSH HOUR EITHER," complained Iris. We were on the Chūō Rapid, our favorite of Tokyo's myriad train lines. Its orange-striped cars arrive at platforms 7 and 8 of Nakano Station every three to four minutes, all day, every day, and it could not be more magical if it left from platform 9¾.

Tokyo is a railroad town. It's hard to say anything about Tokyo trains without resorting to cliches and getting worked up like a fanboy trainspotter. The system is massive: more than one hundred train lines serving nearly nine hundred stations, and you can carry one digital smart card (called PASMO or Suica) that opens the gates to all of them. The heart of the system is the Yamanote line, an above-ground circle line with distinctive green-striped cars that look like life-size toy trains. The Yamanote loop takes about an hour to go all the way around and serves most of Tokyo's most important and best-known stations: Shinjuku, Shibuya, Harajuku, Tokyo, Ueno, and so on.

The Yamanote line carries more passengers per day than the entire London Underground, and it's where Iris and I first encountered crush hour. White-gloved attendants still work in Tokyo train stations, but they no longer push passengers onto trains, because the passengers have mastered the art of, for lack of a better word, self-cramming. Tokyo straphangers are nothing if not orderly. Marks on the platform indicate where the train doors will alight; passengers line up here, step aside to let people off, then sweep onto the train with a minimum of colliding and sniping.

The other day I was on the bus in Seattle. All the seats were taken, and most passengers had to stand. The bus driver kept exhorting people to move toward the back to make room for more passengers. "There's no room to move back," people grumbled. In Tokyo, well, no one complains publicly in the first place, but on any train, no matter how sardined, there's always room to get cozy and make room for a few more. The first time Iris and I found ourselves in the midst of this Vise-Grip of humanity, her face went from relaxed to terrified to elated in the space of ten seconds. In a crush hour train, hands go up. Surrender. As entertainment, it's hard to do better for a $2 ticket.

In the midst of this humid press of bodies, those lucky enough to secure a bench seat tend to celebrate by falling asleep. It's common to look across the train car and see an entire row of people nodding off, like hobos on boxcars, except these are well-dressed, sober professionals of all ages and both sexes, at all times of day. Sleep seems to hunt them down and overtake them. How do they wake up before their stop? I never figured it out. People also sleep in parks. This public narcolepsy is, like a bug-eyed anime doll, both cute and unnerving. Tokyo's subway sleepers square too well with stereotypes about the Japanese working themselves to death. Then again, I fell asleep on the train a few times myself.

The Chūō line cuts east-west across the circle of the Yamanote, forming the London Underground symbol on the idealized transit map. It's a busy line, carrying crush loads in certain places at certain times, but mostly it's just a nice train. Nakano is far enough from the city center that we sometimes even got a seat. I enjoyed the surprisingly comprehensible station and transfer announcements in Japanese and English, and I especially liked the ads. Colorful display ads hawked boring urban stuff like insurance and continuing education and cell phones, but also TV shows like the cop comedy *Beginners* ("BIGINAAZU!") and the romantic drama *Breathless Summer*. A wholesome-looking middle-aged woman starred in a series of ads for bean-flavored popsicles which focused on their health-giving (which I assume means "constipation-relieving") properties.

Each train car featured a TV screen built into the side of the car running mostly food ads. Every time I saw the 7-Eleven ad showing a family gathered around the chain's summer noodle salad, I wanted to be that family, and soon enough, we were. (It was pretty good.) In another ad, a guy in a tuxedo leaned against the counter at McDonald's. I never quite figured out what was going on there. (The commercials don't have audio, just closed captioning, thank God.) Everybody bemoans the omnipresence of commercial messages in modern life; I've certainly asked why we have to give self-interested marketing goons a captive audience on our public conveyances. Tokyo probably has more commercial messages per square foot than anywhere in America, but you know what? It sure beats Poetry on Buses.

Riding the train in Tokyo isn't always a picnic. Some of the newer subway lines, like the Oedo line, are dug insanely deep and require descending an unnervingly long series of escalators to get to the platform. Every time we rode one of these subterranean monstrosities, I thought about the Chilean miners.

Riding the Shinkansen, however, is literally a picnic. Every Shinkansen trip departing Tokyo originates at Tokyo Station, an imposing Renaissance-style building whose main facade somehow survived World War II. Inside, uniformed workers push metal carts stacked with mysterious cardboard boxes up and down the corridors. It's not luggage. Eventually, Laurie figured out that they're delivering bento boxes to the dozens of shops selling them.

Ekiben ("train station bento") are a tradition as old as train travel in Japan. While eating on subways and commuter trains in Tokyo is a bad act, eating on the intercity bullet train is celebrated. There's a hierarchy of bento quality. The kiosks on the train station platforms sell the cheapest and lowest-quality bento, although applying the term "lowest-quality" to any food in Japan is an unfair slur. I've certainly enjoyed these bargain ekiben, which usually contain rice (often decorated with a single umeboshi, said to prevent spoilage and resemble the Japanese flag), pickles, some kind of cooked vegetable or salad, and a main dish like cold fried chicken or tonkatsu or ginger pork or dried fish.

As you get farther from the tracks, the bento become more varied, expensive, and exquisite. If you're feeling flush, you can step outside the station and into a department store, where the basement food halls sell impeccable bento for $30 and up.

My favorite place to shop for train food at Tokyo Station, however, is the deli complex inside the station, which offers a wide variety of bento, plus individual items so you can build your own deconstructed bento, which is what I did on this trip. I bought a box of hot nikuman, which are like those fluffy white steamed Chinese pork buns but with a seasoned ground pork filling instead of gooey barbecued pork, and a plastic tub of assorted root vegetables: kabocha squash, carrots, taro, bamboo shoots, lotus root, burdock, and more, all perfectly cooked and seasoned. Iris had a tonkatsu bento, and Laurie had a fried chicken one that also featured potato salad. She described the combination as "sort of American and totally Japanese."

Another popular train food is the *katsu-sando*, or tonkatsu sandwich, which is a cold pork cutlet with tonkatsu sauce on crustless white bread. I've never been into American cold sandwiches, but sometimes I get a katsu-sando craving.

My stomach hasn't quite come around to the idea of eating lunch while shooting down the track at 180 miles per hour. Most people find the Shinkansen's tracks so highly polished and the trains so aerodynamic and hermetically enclosed that speed is only an idea. My middle ears have never been entirely cooperative, and I find a Shinkansen ride more like being shot out of a cannon. This is not a complaint. It's the bullet train, for God's sake; I want to feel at least a *little* queasy.

About an hour into the ride, we caught a ten-second glimpse of the peak of Mount Fuji, naked of snow in the summertime, and then clouds drew a modest cloak over the mountain and it was gone. That was our only Fuji view of the entire trip. This is also as it should be. Tokyoites, I think, enjoy complaining about not being able to see Mount Fuji much more than they would enjoy being able to see it all the time. Seattleites have the same relationship with the sun.

My favorite part of the Shinkansen experience has nothing to do with food and doesn't even require getting on the train. Stand on the platform in a small town station, and soon an express train will come screaming through at full speed, in and out of the station in five seconds without stopping. The train gives off an earsplitting insect hum. It seems like you're watching something physically impossible, like a person lifting a house, or hearing a joke so funny the laughter threatens to rip you apart, and then, with a puff of air, it's over.

When I was in high school, my friends and I sometimes got bored enough to drive out to the airport to watch planes take off. If it had been a Shinkansen platform, we never would have come home.

Yakitori

焼き鳥

Immediately after the war, underworld gangs opened markets at all three of the mouths [of Shinjuku train station], west, south, and east. Traces of that at West-mouth yet survive, in the cluster of one and two-story "barracks" known popularly and affectionately as Piss Alley (Shomben Yokochō). It would much prefer that the public call it Chicken Alley, for skewered chicken is, along with alcohol, the commodity it chiefly purveys, but the public does not oblige.

—Edward Seidensticker, *Tokyo from Edo to Shōwa*

OUR YAKITORI STORY BEGINS, IN fact, at Piss Alley.

Actually, it begins at our Nakano apartment. One night around bedtime (living in what was basically a one-room apartment meant we almost always went to sleep at the same time), I said good night to Laurie and Iris and headed out into Tokyo. I hopped the express train to Shinjuku, still full of bodies at 9 p.m. and still running every four minutes. I stepped off the train, out of the station and into a warren of chicken shacks that would now prefer that the public call it Omoide Yokochō, or Memory Alley. I'd bet a large bottle of Sapporo that everybody still calls it Piss Alley.

Piss Alley is actually two perpendicular alleys. Tourists and salarymen weave around each other and through clouds of fragrant meat smoke. As I strolled through, I looked for a free seat at a counter and finally took one. "You speak Japanese?" asked the cook. "I don't speak any English."

"That's cool," I said. I did not actually say that. I said, "*Daijōbu desu*," which is pronounced "dye-jobe-dess" and is perhaps the single most useful phrase in Japanese after "*sumimasen*," ("I'm sorry.") Daijōbu desu means I'm OK, it's OK, that's fine, don't worry about it. I said it with confidence despite the fact that I did not, technically, speak Japanese as well as a two-year-old. There were two white guys already at the counter. I figured I could get away with it.

I'd come to Piss Alley to eat chicken, drink beer, and piss in an alley. I only managed one, because (a) I was kidding about pissing in an alley, and (b) I happened to sit down at a pork restaurant. I ordered a bottle of lager, a skewer of pork with negi, and a skewer of zucchini. "Where are you guys from?" I asked the Westerners.

"Belgium," said one.

"Bulgaria," said the other.

It's probably good that I didn't reply, "Those are two different places?" or "You guys must love that Bulgarian drink-able yogurt," because each of these guys weighed about two of me. They worked for a Japanese company, but didn't want to talk about exactly what they did, because that's what you talk about at work, not during pork and beer hour. They asked me how long I'd been in Japan. "A week," I said. This provoked much laughter. They'd been in the country for over two years and didn't seem too happy about it.

The food was excellent and the beer cold. I finished, mar-veling at how much flavor a cook can coax out with a little salt, pepper, and hot charcoal. Sure, it's easy to make pork taste good, but the zucchini was also charred, juicy, and ir-resistible. I wandered around the alley a little more and then out among the skyscrapers and department stores of Shin-juku, thinking about the words of William Gibson. "Shinjuku at night is one of the most deliriously beautiful places in the world," he wrote, "and somehow the silliest of all beautiful places—and the combination is sheer delight."

Yakitori is also sheer delight. On our first trip to Japan, Iris and I went to dinner at a tavern—an *izakaya*—that was part of a national chain and situated invitingly on the bank of the Sumida River in Asakusa. The restaurant had a picture menu, which was a good thing, since neither of us could read any Japanese at the time. Despite the pictures, I managed to order poorly. A chain izakaya is not the place to order sushi, and to drink, I ordered what I thought was a small bottle of sake but turned out to be a small bottle of sake accompanied by a giant bottle of beer. Iris thought this was so hilarious that she still brings it up, three years later.

In retrospect, I'm not sure why I considered unexpected beer a problem, but the place was smoky and not especially welcoming, and Iris was in the mood for tonkatsu but couldn't find any on the menu. She flipped through for a while and then said, "I want *that*."

"Looks good to me," I said. It was some kind of chicken on a stick. When I ordered it, the waiter asked if we wanted *shio* or *tare*. This much I could understand. Shio is salt; tare is a rich, sweet sauce made from reduced soy sauce, mirin, and simmered chicken parts. It's a common choice in yakitori places; tare is the safe option, since anything tastes good with sweetened soy sauce. Salt is for when you really want to see what the grill master can do.

Here we went with tare. Soon the waiter brought two skewers, each loaded up with tiny, glistening bites of chicken. We each took a bite and shared an astonished stare: this was the best chicken we'd ever tasted, and we had absolutely no idea what chicken part we were eating.

Later we figured out that it was *bonjiri* (sometimes written *bonchiri*). In English, it's called chicken tail or, more memorably, the Pope's Nose, a fatty gland usually discarded when prepping a chicken for Western-style cooking. We ordered two more plates of the stuff.

Yakitori is a beak-to-tail approach to chicken. OK, not literally beaks, but common choices at a yakitori place include thigh meat, breast meat, wings, heart, liver, and cartilage. The true test of a yakitori cook, I think, is chicken skin. To thread the skin onto skewers at the proper density and then grill it until juicy but neither overcooked (dry and crusty) or undercooked (unspeakable) requires serious skill.

"I wish we could go somewhere with an English menu so I know what I'm ordering," said Laurie.

"Doubtful," I replied. But I could understand not wanting to leave all the ordering in the hands of, well, me. There was a fifties throwback sexism to it ("And *she'll* have..."), but more to the point, who knows when I might order something weird like chicken skin on a stick?

Laurie got her wish at a yakitori place in Nakano that ended up becoming one of our favorite restaurants. It's a chain restaurant whose actual name is Akiyoshi, but I called it Yakitori Stadium, and Laurie and Iris, picking up on a mistranslation on the English menu, called it Yakitorino. I'll call it that, too, because it's fun to say. The menu was a double-sided laminated (that is, sauce-proof) sheet with Japanese on one side and English on the other.

Diners at Yakitorino sit at a U-shaped wooden counter around the grill, and as the cook finishes grilling each order of skewers, a waiter delivers the food to a heated metal shelf just above the counter. It's a great gimmick. The food is rushed to you as soon as it finishes cooking, and since your fellow customers are eating two feet away on either side, it's easy to spy on and steal their orders. (Order the same thing, I mean, not swipe their skewers, although I certainly thought about it.) When you finish nibbling all the chicken off a skewer, you drop the empty into a black plastic cup, giving a real-time tally of how many you've demolished.

Actually, Laurie only sort of got her wish for an English

menu, because once Iris got her hands on the menu, she took charge. "*Negima onegai shimasu*," she'd say, putting her finger to her lower lip the same way I do when deciding what to order. Negima is the single most popular yakitori skewer, chunks of chicken thigh meat interspersed with lengths of sliced negi.

Charcoal-grilled negi becomes amazingly tender, and the layers slide apart with a nudge of the tooth. Negima is sometimes made in the U.S. with scallions in place of negi, and it's not the same. In general, as much as I like scallions, they make a poor substitute for negi; they're smaller and the flavor is more oniony. American leeks are too tough. I guess the only substitute for negi is dreaming about negi like a nostalgic doofus.

Laurie and I ordered *chūhai* to drink. Short for "*shōchū* highball," chūhai is cheap vodka-like liquor with club soda and often lemon or other fruit flavoring. It's a tall, icy drink, not very strong, perfect for summer. Anyone serious about drinking would dismiss chūhai as being identical to wine coolers, but every drink has its proper context, and a fizzy, unchallenging, lightly alcoholic drink on a hot summer night is hard to beat—especially with salty food.

At Iris's direction, we enjoyed all sorts of skewered bits. While most yakitori places serve various cuts of chicken and a few vegetables, the menu at Yakitorino was all over the place, and nearly everything was good: breaded and fried beef cubes on a stick; fried lotus root; pork jowl with miso; *shishitō* peppers. But Iris and Laurie's single favorite dish at Yakitorino was neither meat nor vegetable and was not served on a stick. "If you'd really left the ordering up to me," Iris said to me recently, "we would have had nothing but *yaki onigiri*."

Yaki onigiri are plain, triangular rice balls (no fillings or nori wrapper) cooked on a hot charcoal grill and brushed with soy sauce or miso. The sauce on the outside caramelizes as the rice becomes charred and crispy and gives off an aroma of popcorn. The interior of the ball heats up and drinks in just a hint of sauce. It is a riot of flavor and texture made with two completely ordinary ingredients.

Iris and I have decided that if we were going to open a Japanese restaurant, it would be a yakitori place, which Iris has dubbed Yakitori Ding-Dong. "You would cook and I would serve," she told me. Which is silly, since I don't know any more about making yakitori than she does, but maybe the knowledge is contained in a master chef's sweaty tenugui. Hand-me-downs, anyone?

Cozy Town

ほっとする

Not much is old in Tokyo, but the street pattern is, and makes Tokyo seem warmer and cozier than Nagoya, a much smaller city.
—Edward Seidensticker, *Tokyo from Edo to Shōwa*

A FEW YEARS AGO I was on a Seattle city board devoted to pedestrian issues. (And let me tell you, we weighed in on some *pedestrian* issues.) A lot of our time was spent advocating for building sidewalks in neighborhoods that didn't have any. Well, most streets in our Tokyo neighborhood of Nakano don't have sidewalks and don't need them.

If you've seen pictures of Tokyo streets, like the teeming Shibuya Crossing or the city's other Times Square–like districts (Shinjuku, Akihabara, and so on), it's easy to get the idea that the whole city looks like that, or that the only respite from urban hyperintensity is to visit a temple or shrine. This is not true at all. Even in the center city districts, if you walk a couple of blocks off the major arterial, the bustle and crush fade quickly.

Tokyo has a bizarre street address system, so arcane that I wouldn't be surprised to learn that it was designed during the Edo period to confuse foreign invaders. Each district is divided into neighborhoods, and each neighborhood is divided into multiblock parcels called *chome* (cho-meh). Within each chome, the blocks are numbered, and on each block, the buildings are numbered. But they're not necessarily numbered in order: building #1 might be between #17 and #24. This means any street address in Tokyo is an incomprehensible string of numbers (building/block/chome). Nobody other than the post office actually navigates by street address; people use landmarks and mobile phones.

My point isn't to scare you away from ever visiting Tokyo, which is actually quite easy to navigate. The reason Tokyo doesn't operate on the lot number/street name system used in American cities is because nonarterial streets in Tokyo, taking a cue from U2, *don't have names.* Our apartment wasn't on Cherry Blossom Lane or any other street with a cute name; like most homes, it was on a nameless street.

As you walk from named to nameless streets, the urban quality changes. The named streets are often huge, packed with cars, with wide sidewalks and tons of street-facing businesses, often several floors of them. It's common, and mouthwatering, to see a tall skinny building with a large sign listing all the restaurants you'll find on its various floors. ("Yakitori

2F, Sushi 3F, Korean BBQ 4F–5F," etc.) The nameless streets are skinny, usually wide enough for one car with room for pedestrians or bikes to squeak by either side of it. Everyone shares the road: parents on bikes with one kid in front and another behind; businessmen in white dress shirts and black slacks (summer "cool biz" style) carrying briefcases; school-girls and schoolboys in uniform; vigorous-looking elderly people; and the occasional slow-moving car or truck. Every time I saw a Domino's or Pizza Hut delivery, I laughed, because the vehicle of choice is a tiny scooter outfitted with a pizza trunk. (Also, I laughed because, hey, why would you order Domino's if you lived in Tokyo?)

No matter how far into the residential area of a neighbor-hood you walk, the side streets are punctuated by vending machines. You've probably heard tales of all the crazy things you can buy in Japanese vending machines, but the golden age of vending diversity, when you could buy sake and books and fetish gear, is mostly gone. Today, nearly all vending ma-chines sell drinks, and in the summer they're indispensable.

Vending innovation isn't dead. Some machines use facial recognition software to guess which drink you're in the mood for (based mostly on your gender and the time of day, I was told). Iris and I always liked to stop at the machine on the Na-kano Station platform that dispensed slushy iced drinks like cocoa-strawberry, matcha, and *Ramune*. (Ramune is a soda known for its unusual bottle, which has a glass marble in the neck, and for coming in various flavors like orange, red, and blue, all of which taste the same to me.)

It took about eighty seconds to shave the ice into the cup,

which meant we'd miss our train. Luckily, the next train was always three minutes behind. We also enjoyed the occasional touch-screen machine, where the screen took up the entirety of the front panel, like a giant iPad, and you'd tap a life-size depiction of the bottle you wanted to buy.

Most vending machines, however, were like the ones in the cluster near our apartment which we dubbed, inventively enough, Vending Machine Corner. For about $1.50, you could get iced green tea or black tea with milk; various sweetened iced coffee drinks like Boss and (actual brand name) Mt. Rainier: The Mountain of Seattle; sports drinks like Speed Athlete and Pocari Sweat; and our personal favorite, water. The iced tea is tasty, but once I made the mistake of trying hot tea from a machine and received a warm plastic bottle. The tea was lousy, but even if it had been the finest first-growth tea from Uji, drinking from warm plastic *will* make you think of a urine sample.

Occasionally we saw someone refilling a machine, but mostly the vending machines were unattended and ready to serve. Where do they plug in? Who owns them? Life is mystery.

Not all of Tokyo's nameless side streets are residential. When we took the Tōbu Tōjō line train deep into Saitama Prefecture to visit friends one Sunday, at every brief station stop along the way we could see a *shōtengai* inviting us to throw out our plans.

A shōtengai is a busy pedestrian shopping street, closed or inhospitable to cars. Walk three blocks down a typical shōtengai, and you'll pass well over a hundred businesses: casual restaurants, convenience stores, record stores, pachinko parlors, used book and record stores, produce stands, clothing shops, all the customary urban mishmash. In Kichijōji one day we took a long detour into a store selling nothing but high-quality clothing buttons, and the place was so charming that even I was into it. My time in that store probably constituted the majority of the time in my entire life I have thought about buttons. On a shōtengai north of Kōenji Station, we ran into a troupe of tipsy comedians mugging for photos.

Years ago I read a quote whose source I've been unable to trace. The writer described great urban spaces "where the city holds you in the palm of its hand." The most important ingredient in that feeling is a pleasant sense of enclosure, of being in what architectural theorist Christopher Alexander calls an *outdoor room*. Tokyo is riddled with this kind of delightful place, and I think it's what Seidensticker was talking about when he said Tokyo's street pattern makes it warm and cozy. Those nameless, narrow backstreets, with frequent intersections and diversions, are Tokyo's fundamental form, and they are arranged into neighborhoods with recognizable personalities.

The Jiyūgaoka neighborhood, for example, can only be described as cute, or, to use the favorite word of every Japanese schoolgirl, *kawaii!* You step out of the train station and into a village of high-end shopping, French bakeries, and international food. Pedestrians mill at train crossings, waiting to let a small commuter train pass, then stream across. On the other side of the tracks is a small strip of park blocks, a bit like

Brooklyn or my hometown of Portland, Oregon. And this is *way* out in the suburbs.

Street patterns are amazingly resilient. Tokyo was destroyed twice in the twentieth century, but an old street map would still serve you well. Visitors to Tokyo have no reason to think about street patterns except to curse them when they get lost, but if Tokyo had been rebuilt along modernist lines after World War II, with a grid system and wide streets, I would not be writing this, because the Tokyo that I love would not exist. Some parts of Tokyo, like the area around Tokyo Tower and some of the artificial islands in Tokyo Bay (like Toyosu and Odaiba) provide an ill-proportioned counterexample to the good urban form that pervades most of the city. I find these areas very hard to appreciate. (OK, they suck.)

But these exceptions are rare, and Tokyo has even found ways to accommodate urban features that provoke hand-wringing and revulsion elsewhere. After an evening walk in our neighborhood of Nakano, Laurie noticed something strange: the three of us had just strolled through an adult entertainment district, and it felt totally family-friendly. "Maid cafes" such as Kuroneco (meaning "black cat" and written in roman characters to be stylish) solicited men looking to spend an evening doted upon by a young woman dressed as a French maid. This is actually more innocent than it sounds— no sex, all doting. Other cafes offered strip shows and possibly more, but as discreetly as you can imagine. There's a strong proscription in Japanese society against belligerent public drunkenness and other forms of public bad behavior, so whatever naughtiness is going on indoors rarely spills over onto the street. There are enough layers of questions (about feminism, sexual openness and repression, and the international appeal of French maids) to build several onions, and I'm not equipped to peel them, but the point is that our neighborhood catered to a variety of urges, gustatory and otherwise, and was safe and comfortable day and night.

(Yes, of course I considered trying the maid cafe, but chickened out because I was worried the language barrier would be embarrassing. In retrospect, I should have gone in wearing a butler costume and we could have had a whole *Remains of the Day* role-play going on.)

Alain de Botton is that guy with a French name who writes books in English about why modern life doesn't make us as happy as it should. He's written books about travel, work, and religion, and a few years ago he wrote a book called *The Architecture of Happiness*. One observation from that book has stuck with me: "[E]ven if the whole of the man-made world could, through relentless effort and sacrifice, be modeled to rival St. Mark's Square, even if we could spend the rest of our lives in the Villa Rotonda or the Glass House, we would still often be in a bad mood."

When you look at a picture of Paris, you want to insert yourself into the scene. That's you, sitting at the cafe, lingering over a croissant and *café crème*. There you are again, on a bicycle, with a baguette sticking out of your satchel. Strolling down the Champs-Élysées. Kissing beside a fountain. Buying macarons in a rainbow of colors. Like it or not, you're the star of *Being Jean-Claude Malkovich*.

Even though Tokyo is a superb place to buy a panoply of macarons, photos of Asian cities don't provoke the same kind of longing, because the cities don't throw up mansard roofs and ornamented terra cotta in the background of every picture. Most photography books and children's picture books about Japan are about Mount Fuji, or Japanese gardens, or something, anything, not marred by power lines.

The great stuff about Tokyo is like a vampire: it doesn't show up in photos. To turn de Botton's observation on its head, we can be very happy living among ugly buildings.

There is, of course, beautiful traditional architecture in Tokyo, just not very much of it, and what looks old often isn't. When we arrived in the city from the airport and emerged from the Ginza line station in Asakusa, our first view was dominated by the Kaminarimon ("thunder") Gate, which marks the entrance to the Sensō-ji temple complex, Tokyo's most visited attraction. The gate, a towering wooden *torii* complete with a hanging red lantern, looks like it has stood guard for a thousand years. This is essentially true: Kaminarimon was built in 941. What you see in 2013, however, is a 1960 reconstruction. (The current red lantern is from 2003.) But most of Tokyo is not reconstructed temple gates. It's soot-stained concrete modernism. And it just doesn't matter.

Tokyo is one of the world's great walking cities. "Walking on the streets of Tokyo we are aware of a sense of human proportion that we might not have known in the cities whence we came," writes Donald Richie in *A Lateral View*. "To walk in Tokyo is to wear a coat that fits exceptionally well." The city assumes you want to enjoy it by foot, bicycle, and train, and it serves up diversions in small doses, like tapas, on every block. As Laurie put it, "Tokyo isn't beautiful at all, but it's full of beautiful things." She didn't know it, but she was echoing Seidensticker, the city's foremost English-language historian. "No one could call the Tokyo of our day a fair city," he wrote, "though it contains beautiful things."

The pretty little thing that jumped out at us all over town, day after day, was the tenugui. Often translated as "washcloth" or "handkerchief," a tenugui is a multipurpose piece of cloth used as a headband, or for brow-mopping on a summer day, or (most often) for drying your hands, because hand-drying implements in public bathrooms are rare. Tenugui are as ancient and folkloric as a hand towel can be. Laurie went to an exhibit of *ukiyo-e* woodcuts and paintings, all of which featured cats, many of which were wearing or otherwise using their tenugui.

Meanwhile, I was reading about Manjirō, the first Japanese visitor to America. Shipwrecked during the Edo period, Manjirō was rescued by an American whaling ship whose captain eventually adopted Manjirō as his son. Manjirō eventually returned to Japan and became a samurai at the dawn of the Meiji restoration. The key part of the story: legend has it that throughout his adventures, *Manjirō never lost his tenugui.* And it's a good thing, because public restrooms in the 19th century almost never had those cool Airblade hand dryers.

Tenugui are for sale everywhere, and each design is more beautiful than the last. Many are both pretty and funny, like the one printed with that eternal symbol of summer, the mosquito coil. At one department store I saw a display of Izod tenugui in rich primary colors, each bearing the little alligator patch. I'm not sure how many tenugui Laurie brought home, but she gave them as gifts for several weeks after our trip, and I have no proof that she's run out.

Maybe washcloths aren't your thing. Fine. Beautiful stuff is inescapable in Japan no matter what your pleasure: temples and shrines, stylish clothing, perfect packaging, grand public gardens and miniature flower gardens sprouting on residential corners, the calligraphic swoop of kanji and the spiky angularity of katakana. And I haven't even mentioned anything food-related. The point is, sure, we all want beauty in our lives, but it doesn't have to come in architectural form.

Then again, the drabness of Tokyo goes a long way toward explaining why people here are obsessed with Paris and, more recently, Seattle. Everywhere we went, we saw ads for direct flights to Seattle on ANA airlines. One of the ads showed our neighborhood bookstore.

Any Tokyoite who visits Seattle will, I'm sure, find it more scenic than their hometown. Given time, however, they'll discover that this matters much less than they think.

Seattle is not an umbrella city. In Seattle, you find tourists by looking under umbrellas. There is more than a little spite underlying the Seattleite's antipathy to standing under an umbrella. If they're going to tell us it rains all the time in Seattle, well, dammit, we can repel it with Gore-Tex and a bad attitude. (Actually, as you're probably tired of hearing by now, it doesn't rain that much in Seattle.)

Tokyo, meanwhile, sprouts umbrellas like mushrooms at the first threat of rain. The most popular umbrella is made of glossy clear vinyl and sells at convenience stores for 500 yen. We accumulated seven umbrellas: three bought on our first day at the FamilyMart; two that came with our apartment, one that Iris and I bought in Ikebukuro after going out umbrella-less, and a child-sized polka-dot umbrella.

"Actually, we had nine," Iris interjected. "Two in Hakone." Oh, right. We spent a rainy day in the mountain resort area of Hakone and left our umbrellas back in Tokyo. More on that later.

It took me weeks to learn how to use an umbrella, and I kept pestering Laurie with Stupid Umbrella Questions and poking people with my umbrella spokes. Luckily, Tokyo is not New York, and people in Tokyo are far too polite to say, "Hey, watch it, fuckface." Slowly, however, I learned the right moment to furl my umbrella in Pretty Good #1 Alley before entering the covered Nakano Sun Mall. And I got used to repairing my umbrella by stuffing a couple of free-swinging naked spoke ends back into their plastic aglets before setting out.

Nearly every establishment in Tokyo offers either an umbrella stand or umbrella bags outside the entrance. One morning, in a downpour, I walked into the Nakano Starbucks with a dripping umbrella and apologetically asked, "*Kasa wa...?*" (What should I do with my umbrella?) An employee ran to the other entrance and brought me a plastic umbrella bag, which I clumsily slipped over my umbrella. I never came close to mastering the umbrella bag, an impressively wasteful device which works like an umbrella condom and is similarly discarded after use. The bottom few inches of my umbrella always pudged out from the opening of the bag like a muffin top.

Tokyo's umbrella culture reaches full flower at Shibuya Crossing on a rainy day. Shibuya Crossing is probably the busiest pedestrian crossing in the world, although a claim like that is hard to verify. (Laurie visited what is allegedly Japan's largest bathroom, a 64-stall behemoth at Venus Fort, a shopping mall designed to resemble Venice and featuring plenty of gaudy statuary and fountains, and a ceiling that mimics the evening sky. Like an American roadside attraction, Japan takes great pleasure in its superlatives.)

In any case, Shibuya Crossing certain *feels* like the busiest. It's a multiway pedestrian scramble; you've probably seen it in photos or in the movie *Lost in Translation*. Every three minutes, the light changes and three thousand pedestrians cross in all directions with amazingly little pushing and shoving, even when you jam three thousand umbrellas into the mix. Cars get trapped in the intersection and pedestrians flow around them like a fluid dynamics simulation. The umbrellas are mostly the clear kombini special, but one in ten is solid color, or striped, or polka dotted, or solid color with two translucent wedges. The slow-moving color umbrellas are like hand-painted frames in a black and white movie. Climb to the second floor of Shibuya Station, or the Starbucks across the street, and you can watch this hypnotic ballet from above.

City life and umbrellas have been partners for a long time, because the modern umbrella is anything but modern: the extendable hub-and-spoke design goes back at least as far as first-century China. You can see this history in the character for "umbrella," which is perhaps the most pictographic of all the kanji:

Like New York, Tokyo's climate is tropical only in the summer. I've been to Thailand, a truly tropical place, where abundant sunlight and water turn into abundant biomass: plants, elephants, and lots of creepy-crawly things, even in the city.

Tokyo doesn't have the weather to produce life quite so exuberantly, but feral cats are a serious, albeit cute, problem, and Laurie and Iris were tormented by mosquitoes which found my flesh mostly unappetizing. (I'm pretty sure actual murders have resulted from someone saying, "Well, I don't have any bites.") And, like any big city, Tokyo has cockroaches.

It was the latter—just one big guy, not an infestation—that chased Laurie and Iris out of the apartment one morning while I was out writing. Iris ran to the bathroom and hid while Laurie trapped the creature and carried it outside. They went to Mister Donut for comfort food, and that's where I met up with them, ate a mochi ring doughnut, and heard the rest of the story.

"And then in the Sun Mall, we saw...I think it was a bat," said Iris.

"I'm sure it was a bird," I replied. "There's no way you're

going to see a bat in the middle of the city in the daytime."

"I guess."

That afternoon we went to Kiddyland, a toy store in Hara-juku specializing in Hello Kitty, Snoopy, and anime characters that haven't yet arrived in America. While walking down Omotesandō-dōri to the store, Iris pointed and said, "Look!" It was unmistakably a bat, flicking its leathery wings as it soared over the busy street from perch to impromptu perch. A bat in flight looks like a stunt pilot having a very bad day. A group of schoolgirls pointed and screamed.

"That's the same bat we saw this morning!" said Iris. "It must have followed me."

I started to say, "I'm sure it's not," but thought better of it.

Tempura

天ぷら

VISITORS TO JAPAN ARE SOMETIMES surprised to find that tempura, the ubiquitous deep-fried side dish in Japanese-American restaurants, can carry a whole restaurant—even a palatial one like the seven-story Aoi Marushin in Asakusa.

Don't get me wrong—tempura is served as a side dish in Tokyo, too, especially at soba and udon restaurants. Step into a branch of the Hanamaru Udon chain, and before you select your bowl of noodles you're confronted with an array of self-serve, a la carte tempura: eggplant, onion, and squash, yes, but also hard-boiled quail eggs on a stick, squid tentacles, or a whole baby octopus. And the way most diners eat their tempura strains the definition of "side dish," because they plunk the crispy morsels right into their noodle broth. Japanese cooks are expert at frying food to a crisp and equally adept at ruining that crispy perfection through dunking, saucing, and refrigeration. I never learned to appreciate a stone-cold, once-crispy pork cutlet, but I enjoy tempura falling apart in hot soup and eaten at the moment when it has taken on broth but maintains a hint of crispness. The ship has hit the iceberg, but it's still momentarily afloat.

The way tempura is meant to be enjoyed, however, is at the counter of a hole-in-the-wall restaurant like Tenta in Nakano. Most tempura restaurants tip their hand via the name of the restaurant. The first character in "tempura" is 天, usually pronounced "ten" and meaning "heavenly." So tempura restaurants are usually called *ten*-this and *ten*-that. This is unnecessary, since you can smell the frying oil a block away. Good tempura restaurants use sesame oil, either alone or mixed with soybean oil, and it's the best-smelling frying oil you can imagine. If I were married to a tempura chef, I would encourage her not to shower after work. Perhaps this is what Napoleon meant when he wrote Josephine, "*Ne te lave pas. J'arrive.*" ("Don't wash. I'll be home soon.")

Tenta is not a destination restaurant. It's a standard neighborhood tempura place, a dive, a bar with eight stools. You come in and order a beer or chūhai, peruse the menu, and tell the chef what you'd like him to fry. The chef at Tenta is a handsome young guy with a round face. He wears a black tenugui to catch the sweat while he works, just one of the many fashions I saw in Tokyo that I'd like to be able to pull off but, Laurie warns, I am the wrong ethnicity. Middle-aged white people enjoy many unfair advantages; the ability to rock brash urban fashion is not one of them.

The chef at Tenta is always smiling, even when he's just been hit with orders for a dozen different types of tempura, many of which require prep work and unique cooking times. For example, one night I ordered *kisu* (a small whitefish, one of Iris's favorites), green pepper, shiitake, shrimp, kabocha squash, and lotus root in rapid-fire succession. He didn't flinch. Before he started cooking, he placed a plate in front of each of us and topped the plates with metal cooling racks so the underside of each piece of tempura would stay crispy. He pulled a length of daikon out of the fridge, grated it on a flat grater, and passed us each a bowl of freshly grated daikon to mix with seasoned soy sauce for dipping. We also had a small plate for gray sea salt.

Tempura chefs mix their batter on the fly. Our guy at Tenta dumped flour into a metal bowl directly from a bag printed with smiling tempura cartoon characters, indicating a low-gluten flour. He added tap water and stirred a few times with chopsticks. Tempura batter is weird stuff: it's not only still lumpy, but it leaves cliffs of dry flour extending up the sides of the bowl. Overmixing is the enemy of good tempura, because it makes the coating tough and chewy, and a confident tempura chef finishes mixing the batter by dragging your shrimp or eggplant through it. By the time the food is cooked, you'd never guess that its crisp and even exterior came from a batter that looks like boarding school cafeteria oatmeal.

Before dipping anything, though, the chef flicks a few droplets of batter into the hot oil with his metal cooking chopsticks to test the oil temperature. Later, after plunging a shrimp into the oil, he'll repeat the motion, flicking batter bits onto the frying food to produce what might be called crispy Klingons.

Iris's favorite item at Tenta is *anago,* sea eel. Unlike its freshwater cousin *unagi,* anago is neither endangered nor expensive. A whole anago at Tenta is about $7.50. I ordered one, and the chef pulled a live eel out of a bucket. It wriggled like, well, an eel. Iris screamed as water droplets flew toward us. The chef managed to wrestle the unruly thing into the sink and knocked it unconscious before driving a spike into its head and filleting it. He unzipped two fillets in seconds. A Provençal saying holds that a fish lives in water and dies in oil; in the world of tempura, a fish can go from watery cradle to oily grave in ten seconds.

Iris loves fried eel meat, dipped in salt, but this is not her favorite part of the anago. After filleting the eel, the chef takes its backbone—*hone* in Japanese—ties it in a simple overhand knot, and tosses it into the frying oil. "Hone," he says, presenting it to Iris, who considers it the ultimate in crispy snack food—and this is a kid who considers taco-flavored Doritos a work of genius (OK, so do I).

One night we ordered a *kakiage,* a silly and sublime fried tempura patty. The chef mixes shredded vegetables (carrots, daikon, burdock, onion, or whatever is on hand) and seafood with loose tempura batter in a small bowl and slides it into the oil. He makes it look easy, but I'm sure if I tried it, my patty would disintegrate and head off, cowering, to the four corners of the fryer. The kakiage is served solo or on a small bowl of rice, drizzled with tempura sauce, and it's light enough to coax apart with chopsticks.

In the U.S., to have a personal relationship with a Japanese chef across the counter, you have to go for sushi. I enjoy sitting at a sushi bar, but there is always the whiff of haute cuisine in the air (or, if you pick the wrong sushi place, the whiff of something worse). You can visit an expensive, artisan tempura counter in Tokyo and order unusual and impeccable seafood, but come on: tempura is fried stuff. You drink frothy mugs of cheap beer and call for more food any time you like. Bacon-wrapped cherry tomatoes on a stick, tempura-fried? Sure, we had that. A bowl of dozens of whole baby sardines, called *shirasu*? Absolutely. (Iris claimed these for herself.) Why aren't there tempura bars in every city in America?

Like tiny restaurants everywhere in the world, Tenta opens whenever the chef is good and ready. We learned not to plan to go there for dinner at our usual 6 p.m. One night we wandered by around 6:30 and were pleased to find the door open, but when we took our seats at the bar, no chef. There was another customer, however, smoking and reading a newspaper.

About fifteen minutes later, the chef walked in and gave a surprised yelp upon finding people in his restaurant. I assume he was asking himself why he left the door open.

Iris ordered her usual anago, looking forward to the fried backbone like a kid who orders a burger but is really all about the fries. The chef presented the knotted bone to her; she picked it up with her chopsticks and promptly dropped it on the floor. She had the stricken look of a kid who has just dropped her ice cream scoop but hasn't started to cry yet: *the world sucks.* We all looked down at the eel bone and wondered what to do. "Give it here," said the chef, in Japanese. I picked the bone up off the floor with my chopsticks and passed it to him. He rinsed it off in the sink, threw it back in the fryer, salted it, and set it on Iris's cooling rack.

"Hone," he said, bowing.

Chains of Love

チェン

IN MY NEIGHBORHOOD IN SEATTLE, I often eat at a Japanese restaurant called Hana. I usually order the beef and onion rice bowl (*gyūdon*) and a couple of pieces of mackerel sushi on the side. The menu also features tempura, udon, soba, salmon teriyaki, gyōza, and a daily bento box.

In Japan, this would be considered the equivalent of a too-many-cooks movie crammed with so many superstars that they didn't bother writing a script. A restaurant with no specialty is a restaurant with no confidence, no guts. There is no Cheesecake Factory in Japan. (There are many restaurants specializing in guts, better known as *naizō ryōri*.)

Ultraspecialized restaurants are becoming popular in the U.S. in the form of food trucks. With a few exceptions like summer street fair fare and roasted sweet potato trucks and fishcake stew (*oden*) carts in winter, Japan doesn't really do street food. Instead, they do tiny and otherwise one-track restaurants.

How specialized do restaurants get in Japan? Every weekday at lunchtime, people queue up on a side street just south of Ningyōchō Station, in an old Tokyo neighborhood. They're waiting to get into Tamahide, a restaurant that serves one dish, *oyakodon*. It is written with the characters for "parent" and "child" and is a runny chicken omelet (get it?) served over rice. There are very few ingredients to this dish: chicken, egg, and rice, soy sauce, mirin, and sugar. There is no vegetarian version, no low-carb salad version, no side dishes other than a tiny dish of pickles perched atop the lid of your bowl. If you're not in the mood for diced chicken meat, however, you can order the dish with chicken liver or ground chicken.

When you make it to the front of the line at Tamahide, you are relieved of your shoes and given a claim tag for them. When I was a kid, I hated wearing shoes more than anything, and I am still deeply skeptical of them. Every time a nice restaurant in Tokyo told me I *had* to take off my shoes, it was a nostalgic thrill.

Diners sit at low communal tables, the kind with the well underneath, not the kind designed to put foreigners' legs to sleep. I joined a pair of middle-aged Japanese women visiting Tokyo and a young guy in summer business attire (white shirt, black slacks) who gave off an unmistakable "don't bother me while I'm eating my chicken" vibe. He ordered the chicken liver bowl, wolfed it down, and dashed out. As in many restaurants, at Tamahide you order and pay at the front before sitting down and leave when you're finished. Japanese restaurants, in general, have carefully eliminated the most stressful elements of eating in restaurants: deciding what to order from a lengthy menu, waiting for the check, tipping, grumpy waiters, oversized portions, wearing shoes (maybe that last one is just me).

A uniformed waitress set down my oyakodon. I took the lid off the red lacquer bowl and inhaled. You eat oyakodon with a spoon, not chopsticks, because eating runny egg and rice with chopsticks would be like a Mr. Bean gag. After the sulky businessman left, the two women and I tried some conversation. I said, "This oyakodon is delicious, isn't it?" but I couldn't understand the response. I told them I was from Seattle and tried to explain that I was in Tokyo for one month; instead, I said, "It's January in Tokyo."

The oyakadon *is* delicious. It's perfectly representative of the subtler side of Japanese food, not the guts side. I dipped my spoon through the omelet and pulled up a scrag of egg, a cube of chicken, and a clump of rice. It was one of those pre-destined combinations, like shrimp and grits, rounded out perfectly by the hint of soy sauce.

I finished my rice bowl and pickles, said goodbye to my fellow tourists, and had an unwelcome reunion with my shoes in the foyer.

Other than chicken and rice, you'll find Tokyo restaurants specializing in fried pork cutlets, curry rice, ramen, udon, soba, gyōza, beef tongue, tempura, takoyaki, yakitori, Korean-style grilled beef, sushi, okonomiyaki, mixed rice dishes, fried chicken, and dozens of other dishes. Furthermore, even if you know something about Japanese food, it's common to come across a restaurant whose menu or plastic food display indicates that it specializes in a particular food you've never seen before and can't quite decipher.

Out of this tradition of single-purpose restaurants, Japan has created homegrown fast-food chains. McDonald's and KFC exist in Tokyo but are outnumbered by Japanese chains like Yoshinoya (beef-and-rice bowl), CoCo Ichiban (curry rice), Hanamaru Udon, Gindaco (takoyaki), Lotteria (burgers), Tenya (tempura), Freshness Burger, Ringer Hut (Nagasaki-style noodles), and Mister Donut (pizza) (just kidding). Of these, only Yoshinoya has U.S. locations, and they're not as good as the ones in Japan, which serve fattier meat. Since the Japanese are generally slim and healthy and I don't know how to read a Japanese newspaper, it was unclear to me whether Japan's fast-food chains are blamed for every social ill, but it seems like it would be hard to pin a high suicide rate on Mister Donut.

Frankly, I couldn't always figure out whether we were eating at a chain restaurant or not. We only realized our favorite yakitori restaurant, Akiyoshi, was a chain after I Googled it. I'm still not clear on the status of Tatsujin, a fried-chicken stand from which we often brought home takeout, nor do I care, because the chicken was so good. Japanese style fried chicken (*tori no karaage*) is somewhere between chicken nuggets and General Tso's chicken: large chunks of boneless dark-meat chicken dredged in starch and double-fried for extra crispiness. Tatsujin makes several flavors of karaage, including original, *"reddo"* (spicy), and these rather disturbing chicken balls called "Juicies," which only Iris liked. A Juicy is a near-perfect fried sphere somehow composed of recognizable slices of oddly juicy chicken meat. If you've ever worried about what might be lurking in your chopped-and-formed chicken nuggets, the alternative may be worse.

To me, the quintessential Japanese chain is MOS Burger. My friend Rob Ketcherside, who lived in Nakano for years before returning to Seattle, is also a fan. "Visitors to Japan always make a big deal about McDonald's teriyaki burgers," said Rob, "but those are a shallow response to what MOS Burger offers." Indeed. MOS Burger serves something resembling a regular hamburger, but it is far beside the point. On one visit to MOS, for example, Iris ordered a Yakiniku Rice Burger, with slices of Korean-style grilled beef between two toasted rice patties acting as a bun. My burger had a regular bun, but the patty was a crispy tonkatsu fillet topped with its usual tomatoey brown sauce. After I finished it, I was still hungry, so I ordered my own rice burger, a vegetarian one filled with *kinpira gobō*, shredded burdock root simmered with soy sauce, mirin, and chiles. Beat that, McDonald's.

Next to the cash register at MOS, I noticed an ad for a new special menu item, only for a limited time: naan tacos. Yes, that would be Indian-style flatbread wrapped around Mexican-style fillings, presumably with a Japanese spin inside and out. I suspect the limited time offer has elapsed by now.

Udon and Soba

うどんとそば

THE BRAIN OF A TOKYOITE, even a short-term visitor, is an twisted mass of three types of noodles: ramen, soba, and udon.

Ramen freaks congregate online to debate noodle texture, toppings, the calibration of fat and salt and seasonings. There is plenty of one-upsmanship in ramen but little in the way of tedious debates about authenticity (at least, not in English). If someone is making a Thai green curry ramen—and someone is—ramen *otaku* will try it and blog about it.

Soba appeals to aesthetes. Ramen is food of the people, as much so in Japan as in any college dorm, and a ramen shop charges more than $10 at its peril. Soba is haute cuisine, and the ultimate soba dish, zaru soba, is precisely the opposite of green curry ramen. It's a tangle of noodles served on a wicker basket. That's it. Maybe some dipping sauce, if the nuttiness of the hand-milled buckwheat isn't enough for you philistines. Soba people don't blog; they communicate through contemplative furrowed brows.

And udon? I don't have a stereotype about udon fans, because udon, at least in Tokyo, is the underappreciated Third Noodle. Ramen is popular throughout Japan, and soba is native to the Kantō region, the Tokyo area.

The chubby, chewy udon noodle hails from Shikoku, the smallest and least populous of Japan's four islands. Udon is hugely popular everywhere—don't get me wrong—but it doesn't provoke idolatry and veneration in Tokyo, just satisfied slurping and chewing.

On its home turf, in Shikoku, however, the Japan Times reports:

> Created by a local designer, Udon No is a character devised as having woken up one morning to find its head filled with udon noodles instead of a brain. It was adopted as the "official ambassador" of an udon producers' association in Takamatsu, the prefectural capital.
>
> "I am the same (as the character) in that the only thing in my brain is udon," said Shigeki Omine, chairman of the association.

Shigeki-san, you and I should hang. Udon is Iris's and my favorite of the three noodles, and I think in part it's because of its accessibility. Udon is really easy to understand. Yeah, there are a few different regional specialties, but basically we're talking about fat wheat noodles in broth.

On our first trip to Japan, Iris and I visited the Fushimi Inari Taisha, the Kyoto shrine known for its thousands of red wooden gates (*torii*) marching up and down a hill. These gates appeared in the movie *Memoirs of a Geisha* and on the cover of countless guidebooks. In person, they're not the least bit disappointing, because the reality dispels any suspicion that someone Photoshopped in most of the gates. You can hike for an hour, literally, through tunnels of torii, and around gate 6237 or so, when hunger begins gnawing, you come upon an udon shack. If the witch from Hansel and Gretel moved to Japan, she'd totally build an udon shack.

The menu is simple: udon in broth, udon in broth with fried tofu...actually, that's all I remember, because udon in broth with fried tofu, *kitsune udon,* is what we were after. The Japanese contend that foxes (*kitsune*) are really into fried tofu. The tofu isn't crispy; it's *aburaage,* the same soft, chewy tofu pockets used to house rice in inarizushi.

If you're making kitsune udon at home, you buy frozen tofu pockets and simmer them in soy sauce and mirin before laying them atop a steaming bowl of udon in a broth made from dashi, soy sauce, and mirin. Garnish with a few scallions, if you like, and that's the dish.

So Iris and I shared a bowl of kitsune udon. Because she was six, many noodles ended up on the floor. (What was my excuse, then?) The tofu acts as a sponge, absorbing broth, mingling the broth with its simmer sauce, and injecting it back into your mouth as you chew. It's similar to the effect of biting into a morel mushroom.

Fortified with udon, we trekked back down the mountain,

pausing to stick our fingers into a stream running alongside a steep staircase and to take many touristy photos.

That was our temple udon experience, but udon in Tokyo serves much the same function. You've been lost among seductive streets and alleys for too long, and it's time for lunch. What to eat? Udon. It will be cheap, good, and unchallenging. In fact, my single favorite dish of our entire Tokyo summer was served at an udon chain restaurant.

Hanamaru Udon is a popular noodle chain with many locations throughout Japan, including one on Nakano-dōri near our apartment. It was, I suspect, the inspiration for the Wagamama noodle shops in England. The Nakano location is at the bottom of a steep, narrow staircase and through a door into a pleasant mess hall with a counter up front and long communal tables.

The menu features a bunch of classic udon dishes like kitsune, on-tama (with a soft-boiled egg), and Iris's favorite, *kake udon*, which is noodles in broth and nothing else, the Japanese equivalent of buttered noodles with Parmesan from the kid's menu. Fast-food udon is as cheap as American fast food and immeasurably tastier: Iris's small kake udon cost less than $1.50. When she ordered it, the cook picked up a bowl, added hot noodles, and then filled it with broth from the spigot of a large dispenser. (In the dining area was a dispenser for complimentary *genmaicha* tea and another that emitted ice and water simultaneously through the same orifice, which Iris and I could not stop playing with.)

Every noodle bowl at Hanamaru is available in three sizes; the large is sized for sharing or sumo wrestlers. That said,

I frequently saw Guinness-worthy feats of eating in Tokyo. This is a stereotype more closely associated with America, I know, and it's true that food in Tokyo was served in less gargantuan proportions than back home. It was fascinating but not unusual, however, when the grandmotherly woman across from me one afternoon at Hanamaru Udon ordered a huge combination meal with a big noodle bowl, a serving of curry rice, and a few pieces of tempura—a lunch I could not have finished at gunpoint. She ate everything patiently and neatly. It was kind of beautiful.

Now, the greatest dish of summer: spicy *sudachi* udon.

Japan grows a Destiny's Child-like trio of small, yummy citrus fruits: *yuzu, kabosu,* and sudachi. Yuzu is the only one widely (and not that widely) known outside of Japan. All are sour and taste like successive pulsating flavor waves of lime, lemon, and mandarin orange. Sudachi are adorably tiny and round, like key limes.

Spicy sudachi udon is a bowl of cold udon topped with grated daikon, sliced negi, minced spicy green chile (cooked by steaming or boiling, I think), and a halved sudachi for liberal squeezing. Nothing I ate in the course of a month in Tokyo tasted more Japanese or was a more perfect antidote to Tokyo's appalling summer weather. As much as I love hot udon (with fried tofu, or curry, or pork and miso, or stir-fried with chicken and cabbage and fish flakes), thick noodles achieve their chewiest inner perfection when served cold.

I ate this dish for breakfast, lunch, and dinner, though not on the same day. I loved it so much, I did my best to recreate it at home. Here is the only recipe in this book:

SPICY KEY LIME UDON

Adapted from Hanamaru Udon

Serves 2

Mentsuyu is a sauce base used in a variety of noodle dishes. You can make it at home, but since you're probably going to a Japanese grocery anyway for other ingredients, you can buy it premade, in the soy sauce or dried noodle aisle. It's usually sold in a milk carton. If you want to make mentsuyu, I recommend the recipe at japanesecooking101.com, but any recipe you find online should be fine. If you like less spice, remove the seeds and ribs from the jalapeño before mincing.

  1 Anaheim chile
  1 jalapeño chile
  Salt
  2 blocks frozen udon (1 pound total)
  1/4 cup grated daikon
  1/2 cup sliced negi (or 1/4 cup sliced scallions)
  6 tablespoons mentsuyu
  2 key limes, halved

1. Bring a large pot of water to a boil.

2. While water is heating, roast the chiles under the broiler, 5 minutes per side, or carefully over a gas flame, until the skins blacken. Let the chiles cool on a plate for ten minutes, and then discard the stem, seeds, and ribs, and skin of the Anaheim chile; discard the stem

and skin of the jalapeño. Mince the chiles and combine, seasoning lightly with salt.

3. Add the blocks of frozen udon to the boiling water (no need to thaw the udon before boiling), return to a boil, and boil 1 minute, stirring frequently to loosen the noodle mass. Drain and rinse well with cold water.

4. Divide the noodles between two large soup bowls. Top each bowl with half the daikon, chile mixture, and negi, arranging the toppings in three distinct mounds. Pour 3 tablespoons mentsuyu into each bowl. Serve with key limes; squeeze the lime halves over the noodles and stir everything together well before eating.

Eventually I worked up the courage to join the salarymen (and occasional woman) for breakfast at the nonchain noodle stand across from Nakano Station. The noodle stand has a yellow awning reading INAKA SOBA UDON. I'm not sure whether Inaka ("country-style") is the name of the place or just a description of the fare.

The noodle place can accommodate six diners, standing room only. You wait for a spot to open up at the counter, poke your head under the *noren,* and order fast. It's not a place you walk into; you're literally standing on the street while you eat. I scouted the joint for several days, trying to read snippets of the menu as I walked past, because I didn't want to be the stammering foreigner holding up the line, or, worse, the self-important foodie who wants to discuss every aspect of the menu while everyone else is just trying to get to work.

Now that I've had my breakfast, I can tell you how it's done. You will be shocked to learn that Inaka Soba Udon serves two dishes: soba and udon. You call out your noodle of choice, which is quickly refreshed in hot water and tossed into a pottery bowl, where it gets a ladle of noodle broth—heavy on the soy sauce—and a handful of sliced negi.

The trick is in the toppings. The menu at Inaka is just a list of potential additions to your noodle bowl. I took a quick look left and right, saw a kakiage (vegetable tempura cake) luxuriating in a neighboring bowl, and requested one for my soba, plus a raw egg. The serving process takes about ten seconds and is presided over by an old woman who I assume is the owner; she didn't cook while I was there, but she takes the money and makes sure everything runs smoothly. You hand over the cash while the cook makes your noodles; that way you can run for the train as soon as you finish. My soup was 420 yen, about $5. Other popular toppings are kitsune and *chikuwa*, a sausagelike tube of fish paste which is tastier than it sounds.

My soba arrived steaming hot and fragrant. I haven't figured out how to eat Japanese noodles anything like a native. When I slurp, it makes the wrong kind of noise, and I'm always biting off noodles and letting them drop back into the bowl, which is a no-no. Furthermore, I looked down the counter and noticed I was the only one accumulating a palette of broth droplets in a six-inch radius around my bowl, which the owner occasionally wiped away with a towel. The kakiage became reassuringly saturated with broth, and I broke my egg yolk and stirred the egg into the soup. My favorite part of the meal was lifting the bowl to my mouth and drinking the broth, rich from egg and tempura grease and noodle starch. It was sturdy enough to fortify me for several hours of intense writing.

That's not a joke. Really! This was the first morning I didn't find myself dreaming of Mister Donut around 9:30. I ate my soup as fast as I could but it wasn't fast enough. The guy at the end of the counter who came in after me and, I was pleased to note, ordered the same thing I did, finished his soup before me and ordered a second bowl. The portions at Inaka are country-style. A second bowl would have killed me, but then, I was just walking a block to the Starbucks, not dashing for the Chūō Rapid and a day of meetings and pie charts and, uh, whatever it is businesspeople do.

For more hands-on udon experience, all three of us signed up for an udon-making class with Elizabeth Andoh. Actually, "hands-on" is a misnomer, because udon dough is too stiff to knead with your hands. Home udon-making, it turns out, has something in common with traditional winemaking.

Andoh is the Julia Child or Diana Kennedy of Japanese food. Originally a New Yorker, she married an executive at the Takashimaya department store decades ago and found her calling writing cookbooks and teaching classes about the food of her adopted home. She reminds me a lot of my mother and other members of my very New York Jewish family: never at a loss for words, convinced that there is a right way to do something, and why would you bother with any other way?

The udon class was for kids and parents, and the kids who showed up included a studious Canadian teenager, a boy Iris's age from the Philippines, and a couple of lively American boys. We nibbled on rice crackers and udon toppings (the kids were especially interested in tasting chikuwa, the fish sausage, which doesn't taste like much but slices into cool rings that you can slip onto fingertips like olives). Andoh walked us through making homemade dashi with kelp and bonito flakes, and then the kids stirred together whole wheat flour, water, and salt for udon dough.

The dough went into Ziploc bags and the kids stomped it into submission with stocking feet. If you're looking for a way to bring together children of various ages and cultures, put them to work stomping on something. Alternatively, slip them parental smartphones during a break. Iris and the Filipino kid took turns playing a game called Jetpack Joyride, and each seemed surprised that the other was familiar with the game.

Iris was put in charge of grating daikon, and she went at it with gusto, shaving down a thick radish stalk into smooth *oroshi* on a flat, circular grater. The kids rolled out and sliced their noodle dough, and we ate cold udon and hot udon. Kid-made udon noodles are especially chubby and rustic, varying in thickness and length, somewhere between noodles and spätzle. The whole wheat flour married well with the sauce, which was our homemade dashi plus soy sauce, sake, and mirin. Each kid and adult selected a chopstick rest from Andoh's massive collection (Iris took a sumo wrestler; I went with a chile pepper) and applied their choice of toppings: sesame seeds, negi, daikon, chikuwa. I chose some of everything.

In the movie *Tortilla Soup,* an American retelling of Ang Lee's classic *Eat Drink Man Woman,* the family comes together at the end to eat the title dish, and during an awkward silence, the Paul Rodriguez character quips, "I just love toppings." It's one of my favorite lines in any movie, ever, and to get sentimental about it, people may prefer different toppings, but we're all udon and sauce underneath.

While we ate, one of the parents asked Andoh what American foods she craved. "Nothing, really," she replied. "You know, I've lived in Japan for almost *fifty years.*" She sounded surprised about it herself.

By the end of our Tokyo summer, I wasn't missing any American foods either, although I did have a craving for spicy food, which is too rare in Tokyo. I think one lobe of my brain runs on capsaicin. One day I almost stepped in front of a car while leering at an ad for a spicy Middle Eastern sandwich. It's a good thing I discovered spicy sudachi udon.

Katakana Accent

カタカナ

A MONTH BEFORE OUR TRIP, my friend Henry asked me what I was most looking forward to eating in Japan.

"Where do I begin?" I replied. "There's ramen, yakitori..."

Henry interrupted me with a look that said, unmistakably, "You are the biggest dork." I'd been saying the names of common foods in an exaggerated accent, like an American news anchor pronouncing "Nicaragua."

I did my best to break this annoying habit. Once we got to Tokyo, however, I had to pick up an even stranger habit: *pronouncing English words in a way that would be totally racist back home.*

When I studied French in high school, we learned that France has a snooty (even by French standards) government department charged with maintaining the purity of the language and defending it from foreign interlopers like *le meeting* and *faire du camping.* This effort has mostly failed, of course, but there have been occasional successes, like *l'ordinateur* for "computer," instead of, perhaps, *le computeur.*

Japan hasn't even tried. Japanese is so full of English words, it reads like a bicultural ransom note. Those English words, along with some assorted French, German, Portuguese, and recently borrowed Chinese words, are rendered in katakana. For example, here's how you say "computer" in Japanese:

コンピューター

which is pronounced "kompyuutaa."

An English-speaker in Japan will spend a hilarious amount of time saying English words recast in Japanese phonemes. One day I was waiting in line for ice cream with my friend Kate, who speaks Japanese, and asked her which of the many words for "small" I should use when ordering a small cone. I didn't want to commit the equivalent of walking into a Cleveland Baskin-Robbins and ordering a petite uni-scoop cone.

"I'd just say *sumōru,*" she replied. Sure enough: I asked for a "*sumōru kōn, chokoreito,*" and got exactly what I was after: a small cone, chocolate.

These English loanwords—thousands and thousands of them—sound the way they do because, compared with English, Japanese has a limited range of allowable syllables. I once took a Japanese class and sat next to a guy named Carl. That's a very hard thing to say in Japanese. There's no distinction between *r* and *l,* and consonants generally aren't allowed to cluster. When an English word is imported to Japan, it has to be unpacked, translated into Japanese sounds, and written in *katakana,* the alphabet used for writing foreign words.

Carl, at best, turns into *Kaaru*.

This unpacking and repacking of words reminded me of something, but I couldn't figure out what it was until I was watching Iris play with Legos one day. Lego blocks come in a limited number of shapes and colors, but you can build anything with them: a castle, a police station, Mount Rushmore. When you finish and take a step back from your creation, yes, it looks like Abraham Lincoln, but it never stops looking like Legos. English words in Japanese are like that, too. They sound something like the original, but are built from a new toolbox of parts, just like the way Japanese cooks disassembled Western foods and reassembled them in the form of yōshoku.

Throwing around English words with a katakana accent was lots of fun. I tried it any time I didn't know the name of something in Japanese, with nearly total success. Pancakes? *Pankēki*. Beer? *Bīru*. Culture shock? *Karuchā shokku*.

Understanding the response to my request? That's another story.

Every time I've traveled to a non-Anglophone country, it's been like pulling up to a fast-food drive-through. You give your order and are rewarded with a barrage of incomprehensible static. Please drive forward!

I've walked into the same scenario in Japan, Thailand, and France. (At least the food was better than drive-through quality.) My mouth is pretty good at producing sounds in other languages. I can say the French *r* and the Japanese *r/l* and the Spanish...why is it always the *r*, anyway?

It's not that people take me for a suave native speaker. My American accent comes with me as if I packed it in my suitcase. But they can tell I'm trying. My attempts to speak are proficient enough that they don't come across as the usual foreigner's cry for help: *Please put me out of my misery so we can switch to English, already!*

So I ask, confidently, "Where's the bathroom?" (Incidentally, the most common word for "bathroom" in Japanese is an English loanword: *toire,* derived from, yes, "toilet.") But if the reply is anything more complicated than a pointed finger, I have to put on my linguistic dunce cap and say, "Sorry, I don't understand."

I'm ashamed of this. I love unraveling a mystery, and a language is a box of moving parts. How do they work together? What are the rules and the exceptions?

These puzzle-box aspects of language also, as it happens, had an intuitive appeal to the proto-geeks who invented modern computing. A geek's got to eat, and as Steven Levy explains in his book *Hackers,* MIT computer scientists fueled their nocturnal coding sessions the same way their counterparts here and abroad do today, with Chinese food.

> Chinese food was a system, too, and the hacker curiosity was applied to that system as assiduously as to a new LISP compiler.... They went back loaded with Chinese dictionaries and demanded a Chinese menu. The chef, a Mr. Wong, reluctantly complied, and Gosper, Samson, and the others pored over the menu as if it were an instruction set for a new machine. Samson supplied

the translations, which were positively revelatory. What was called "Beef with Tomato" on the English menu had a literal meaning of Barbarian Eggplant Cowpork. "Wonton" had a Chinese equivalent of Cloud Gulp.

In the seventies, Calvin Trillin wrote about his fantasy of eating in New York's Chinatown accompanied by Mao Tse-Tung. Trillin had no sympathy for Mao's politics (also, Mao was already dead at the time); he just wanted the Chairman's help translating the specials written in Chinese and posted on restaurant walls. He should have just brought some hackers from NYU.

Cut to Tokyo. For the first two weeks of our trip, I was in full-on drive-through mode. I couldn't understand two-word responses. Eventually, the language started to click. As a verbal fusillade approached, I pared off honorific prefixes and verb endings and focused on the key words: *Ah, she said "nomimono." She's asking me what I want to drink! Also, she's holding up a glass and gesturing wildly at it*. When I successfully parsed a sentence, it felt like someone threw a fish at me and I filleted it in midair.

I never got good at speaking Japanese and never got better than your average Japanese baby at understanding it. But I managed to pull off one feat that eludes Calvin Trillin and Japanese babies alike: I learned to read.

Japanese has four writing systems.

Let me say that again. *Japanese has four writing systems.* If you want to read and write it fluently, you have to learn four writing systems. This is like being told that if you want to pass the driving test, you will have to build a car from scratch, and that car will have to pass California emissions standards.

Luckily, three of the writing systems are easy. One is the good old Roman alphabet. The other two, *hiragana* and katakana, are easy to learn and easy to recognize. Hiragana is squiggly and cuddly-looking; katakana looks like ninja weapons.

Katakana, as I mentioned, is used to write foreign words. This isn't its only use, but it's by far the most common. Learning katakana should be on the to-do list of every traveler to Japan. It takes a week to learn and will allow you to read all sorts of product names, signs, and menu items. Hiragana is not especially useful without its scary big sister, *kanji*.

Kanji are the complex characters, originally from China, used for writing most Japanese words. Think of the Chinese side of a Chinese restaurant menu. That's kanji.

Learning kanji is an ultramarathon of the mind. Students in Japan begin studying kanji in kindergarten and finish, two thousand–plus characters later, in high school. Imagine sitting in high school English class and learning new letters of the alphabet. Thinking about it makes me want to fling spitballs.

Chinese characters are often described as pictographic. A few of them are, like rain (雨), mouth (口), rice field (田), woman (女), and mother (母, which theoretically looks like breasts if you turn your head sideways; was this the original emoticon?). The rest are intricate assortments of symbols that have little or nothing to do with the concept denoted by the character. For example, 新 means "new." Why? Who knows? Kanji are properly known as *ideographs,* not pictographs, because each one represents an idea, and because learning them makes you feel like an ideot. (Sorry.)

Now, I don't mean to hold myself out as a Kevin Costner-like folk hero who charmed the natives with his knowledge of their impenetrable writing system. I didn't actually learn enough kanji to read a book. Essentially, I cheated, and I did so in a way that highlights one of the most bizarre features of an ideographic writing system: understanding without reading.

To attack the kanji, I used a controversial book called *Remembering the Kanji,* by James Heisig. RTK, as it is known by its adherents (a fringe group of international businesspeople, manga geeks, and guys looking to meet Japanese girls), teaches kanji via mnemonic stories. You take all the little bits and pieces in each character and arrange them into a vignette—preferably something violent or sexy, like all good mnemonics. By the end of the book, you've learned the meaning of all the common kanji—*but none of the pronunciations.* (Each kanji can have multiple, totally unrelated pronunciations; most have at least two.)

And that's where I found myself when we arrived in Tokyo. I could read hundreds or thousands of words in the sense of understanding their meaning, but without the slightest idea of how to pronounce them. (English pronunciation is notoriously difficult, but this is another category altogether.) It turns out that this level of functional (il)literacy, while not ideal, is extremely handy. If you're looking for the south exit and see a sign that says 南口 ("south mouth"), who cares if you can actually pronounce it?

Most important, I could read menus, including izakaya menus, which are generally posted on vertical wooden strips on the wall of the restaurant. I wasn't fast, but I was good enough. If I couldn't pronounce, I could point. (The names of many ingredients and dishes are written in hiragana or katakana, which made navigating a menu even easier.)

One delightful side effect of an ideographic writing system is that there is no need for a distinction between words and symbols. In English we call our money "dollars" but usually write it as $. In Japanese, the word for "yen" and the symbol are one and the same: 円. So it goes for tin cans (缶), men's and women's bathrooms (男 and 女), paper (紙), books (本), and ice (氷). The last is just the kanji for water (水) with a tiny extra shard to tell you it's frozen.

I'm a long way from learning how to pronounce most kanji and understanding the myriad ways they combine into words, and I still think it's the most annoying writing system ever devised. The more time I spend with these characters, however, the more I start to resemble the female lead at the beginning of a romantic comedy: *That writing system is so annoying! Why can't I stop thinking about it? Probably because it's just so annoying. It's not that I'm in love with kanji or anything.*

Sushi

寿司

AT THE BEGINNING OF OUR trip, we met up with a friend from Seattle, traveling with his teenage daughter, and he regaled us with tales of sushi meals. As he told it, it sounded like they'd made their way through Honshu, mouths agape like baleen whales, vacuuming up sushi wherever they found it: an unexpected piece of beef sushi high in the Japanese Alps, a blowout *omakase* meal in Shibuya, and many others.

Well, sorry, Bruce. I ate very little sushi in Tokyo. I didn't try for a reservation at the Michelin three-star restaurant run by Jiro Ono and featured in the documentary *Jiro Dreams of Sushi*, or the restaurant run by Jiro's son, or any of his competitors who wish they were in a movie but have to settle for the fact that people will pay $350 and up to eat their sushi.

I did have several sushi meals, including one *omakase* (chef's choice) dinner at a well-regarded neighborhood joint where the meal ended with a lovely miso soup full of meaty fish bones. And, of course, we went for *kaitenzushi*, conveyor belt sushi, where the food travels around on a motor-driven belt. I've been taking Iris for conveyor belt sushi since she was three; there's a popular chain in Seattle that caters to children by stocking the belt with things like cream puffs and miniature doughnuts and fried chicken. At Tokyo chains like Sushi-Go-Round, it's all sushi and beer. Oh, and I loved seeing colorful pieces of *nigiri* sushi, fingers of rice topped with a slice of fish, individually wrapped in cellophane for sale at the deli in the basement of Nakano Broadway.

Every time I ate sushi in Tokyo, however, it reminded me of Seattle. The number one question people asked us when they learned where we were from was, "Do people eat Japanese food in Seattle?" And I would explain, every time, that in Seattle, Japanese food is synonymous with sushi. Some people had heard of this phenomenon. Most found it perplexing, as if American food had taken root abroad but only in the form of lobster rolls. (I got big laughs by adding that the entire city of Seattle has about five ramen shops and one udon shop.)

Seattle does a pretty good job with sushi. Our hometown sushi hero, Shiro Kashiba, studied under Jiro Ono, and his eponymous restaurant, Shiro's, is world-class. We also have plenty of good, cheap sushi. Every time I had sushi in Tokyo, it felt like a wasted meal, not because there was anything wrong with the food but because Tokyo is packed with amazing food unavailable within four thousand miles of Seattle.

This is grumpy, I know, and to be a stickler, I probably

should have gone to one of the famous $350 places to see what the fuss is about, although for the same price I could visit thirty-five ramen shops. But I did have one memorable only-in-Japan meal of raw fish and rice. It happened at 8 a.m.

Tsukiji is Tokyo's fish market and also the Tokyo *of* fish markets: bigger and fresher than everyone else put together. It's a popular tourist attraction, but it greets visitors with a Goofus and Gallant–style cartoon plaque showing you how not to behave, followed by a walk through a loading area where you'll star in a life-sized game of Frogger, dodging forklifts and little trucks shuffling coolers of snapper, tuna, octopus, shellfish, and ugly, tasty things with no English names.

We woke Iris up at 6:30 a.m. to head to Tsukiji, a dire trip across town on the most depressing of Tokyo's subway lines. By the time we got there, Iris was hungry and cranky and not exactly in the mood for sushi. A shopkeeper noticed her morning face and offered a solution in the form of *monaka,* a Japanese ice cream treat of vanilla ice cream sandwiched between waffle-like cookie layers. It's the least messy ice cream treat in the pantheon, so naturally Iris pried it open to get at the good stuff and ended up with sticky digits. The shopkeeper, smiling, invited Iris into the back of her shop so she could wash her hands.

Thus fortified, we wandered aimlessly around Tsukiji, squinting at a map and at the displays of seaweed, knives, tea, and utensils. (The actual fish is sold in the inner market, which comes to life around 3am.) We circled past the two famous sushi counters (Dai and Daiwa) and their queues of bloodshot tourists, settling on a place specializing in *kaisendon,* sashimi rice bowls. If you're familiar with *chirashizushi,* with various types of fish scattered over a bowl of rice, kaisendon is similar. I ordered a fatty tuna bowl; Laurie ordered salmon; and Iris ordered the one cooked dish on the menu, gigantic fried shrimp (*o-ebi furai*). Even post-ice cream, she wasn't ready for raw fish, but heads-and-all shrimp? No problem.

Eating at Tsukiji is more about the atmosphere than the food, although the ruby slices of fish and well-seasoned sushi rice were more than adequate. The place was as glamorous as a New York coffeeshop, with a half-assed Hawaiian decor and gruff counterman pouring bottomless cups of hot barley tea. I enjoyed watching Laurie power through a bowl of sashimi, one of her least-favorite foods, and then say, "Well, I ate sushi for breakfast at Tsukiji fish market. Didn't I?" I'm not sure what character flaw makes me relish this sort of thing; analyze away. I also like watching Jews eat bacon.

Steakhouse vs. Porkhouse

JAPAN ISN'T MEAT-CRAZED IN THE same way as the USA, but when the Japanese want meat, they want it as marbled as the Parthenon. The most popular topping for ramen is pork belly, streaked with fat, rolled up like pancetta and braised for hours in pork broth until fall-apart tender, then sliced into a perfect round.

One day, Iris and I took the train to Kichijōji, a hip neighborhood in western Tokyo, in search of lunch at Satou Steakhouse. Because Satou serves high-quality meat at reasonable prices, there's often a line, and when we arrived, sure enough, there was a line. Standing in line is something of a national sport in Japan, and people do it with fortitude and a smile. This line, furthermore, was in a lively shopping arcade and adjacent to many other meat-oriented restaurants, which seemed like a good business plan. Iris read *Anne of Green Ga-*

bles while we queued.

One of the most frustrating aspects of being linguistically challenged is never knowing when you're in the wrong line. We were in the wrong line. These folks were waiting to get their hands on menchikatsu, an artisan-quality version of the panko-breaded hamburger patty popular at convenience stores. Luckily, it only took us fifteen minutes to figure this out. There was almost no line at the restaurant, up a steep flight more ladder than staircase. The lunch menu had only three options, all of them steak.

Every seat at the steakhouse has a view of the griddle, where intense cooks fret over each piece of meat, seasoning it well with salt and pepper and occasionally covering the steak with a copper lid. I hesitate to even bring this up, but if you've been to Benihana, subtract the knife-juggling theatrics and you understand the basic idea of a Japanese *teppanyaki* steakhouse. The cooks cut your steak into chopstick-friendly cubes and serve it alongside a big pile of sauteed bean sprouts, moistened with the meat juices. Iris wasn't interested in the bean sprouts, which was great, because I couldn't stop eating them.

The steak, from seasoning to flavor to presentation to portion size, was perfect. Rather than aiming for a deeply charred crust, the cooks at Satou concentrate on juiciness and texture throughout.

And they do it with cuts of meat not worth eating in America. Iris and I were eating round steak, which in the U.S. is always lean, tough, and meant for the grinder at best. Here, though, the meat is so thoroughly marbled, even these lesser steaks become great.

"If I were a vegetarian, this piece of steak would make me start eating meat," said Iris, poking at a particularly rare chunk with her chopstick.

On another day, we walked through Harajuku and onto Omotesandō-dōri, a high-fashion shopping street lined with shops I'd never heard of, selling clothes that wouldn't fit me, at prices I couldn't afford.

We turned onto a residential street near the Omotesando Hills shopping mall and stepped into a tonkatsu restaurant called Maisen. The menu promised pork tender enough to cut with chopsticks, which struck me as a polite way to say, "Fork-tender? Nice try, Americans."

Tonkatsu restaurants, even cheap fast-food ones, offer a choice of *hire* ("fillet") or *rosu* ("roast") pork. Hire is leaner; rosu is fattier. At fancier tonkatsu places, like this one, there is also a choice of various heirloom and otherwise fancy pork breeds, such as kurobuta, Spanish Iberico, or Tokyo-X, a breed developed by the Tokyo Metropolitan Livestock Experiment Station, which is a real thing. Iris and I just ordered the basic rosu. Like all tonkatsu, it's sliced into strips and presented on a small metal rack so the underside doesn't get soggy. The first thing we did, naturally, was try to cut the meat with chopsticks. We succeeded. The pork was juicy, the coating well-seasoned and fried to crispness.

The tonkatsu came with pickles, miso soup, rice, house-made tonkatsu sauce, and a mound of thinly shredded cabbage—not napa cabbage but the same sturdy green cabbage sold at every American supermarket. These are all common accompaniments to tonkatsu, but the cabbage is considered mandatory, and a waiter came around frequently with a pair of tongs and a giant platter of cabbage, ready to replenish our stock, and seemed slightly disappointed that nobody had finished their cruciferous Everest. Cabbage Replenisher would be a great Japanese Halloween costume; everyone would recognize it immediately. ("Cabbage replenisher" is also super-fun to sing in a guttural death metal voice.)

If you enjoy pork and have never made tonkatsu, I encourage you to give it a try. It's easy to make at home and doesn't require deep-frying. Tonkatsu shallow-fried in half an inch of oil is just as good. A dinner of tonkatsu, short-grain rice, store-bought Japanese pickles, and shredded cabbage is a very Tokyo thing.

Hot Pots

鍋物

IT'S DISAPPOINTING BUT INEVITABLE THAT one serving of *chanko nabe* ("knob-eh") will not turn you into a sumo wrestler. At least, it didn't work for me.

Ryōgoku is Tokyo's sumo district. The country's foremost sumo stadium is here, its appetite for wrestling talent fed by neighboring sumo training stables—a term I did not make up and which seems unfair to sumo wrestlers, who are stronger than draft horses.

We were in Ryōgoku to meet our friends Wade (dad) and Joseph (four-year-old) at the Edo-Tokyo Museum, an imposing modern structure that looks sort of like an AT-AT from *The Empire Strikes Back*. At any moment, the building could spring to life and tromp westward, modern Tokyo trampled by historic Tokyo. Since the history of Tokyo is substantially the history of things falling down and catching fire, this wouldn't be so surprising. Iris and I admired a ten-foot-tall replica of the Twelve Stories, an early skyscraper built in Asakusa in 1890. It was an instant hit among locals and a symbol of the neighborhood until it died young like a movie idol, toppled by the Great Kantō Earthquake in 1923.

The Edo-Tokyo Museum thoughtfully provides small, hands-on metal models of the Twelve Stories and other structures for its visually impaired patrons. Less thoughtfully, the museum uses the phrase, referring to 1941, "The Pacific War broke out that fall." Gosh, how'd that happen?

After getting our fill of Tokyo history, we headed down the street to fill up sumo-style. Chanko nabe, like all hot pot dishes, is cooked on the tabletop and eaten communally, with diners transferring choice bits from the hot pot to their own small bowls. The genuine sumo version is a humble chicken and vegetable stew. The use of chicken is part nutrition and part superstition: chickens walk on two feet, and a wrestler knocked off his feet loses the sumo match.

At the eight-story chanko house across from Ryōgoku Station, it's a little more upscale. You'll find pork belly, shrimp, scallops, meatballs, fish balls, shiitake mushrooms, and two kinds of tofu in the nabe. We ordered hot pot for two, guessing correctly that this would serve three adults and two children.

It was a 90-degree day, and eating a steaming hot pot on such a day sounds like following a sign reading WELCOME TO HELL—VISIT OUR NEW BASEMENT! On the fourth floor of an air-conditioned restaurant, however, with a view of the SkyTree and the Sobu line trains streaming in and out of Ryōgoku Station, chanko is fine any day. The pot arrived with all the ingredients inside except for the pork meatballs, which came in the form of seasoned raw ground pork in an abalone shell. With a spoon, our waiter formed a small ball and dropped it into the shōyu- and dashi-based broth, which was beginning to bubble. He let Iris make the final meatball, which she immediately became attached to, warning the rest of us to keep our chopsticks off her meatball.

The best part of chanko nabe is near the end, when the best bits are long gone and the pot contains an intense stock, heavily reduced and a little greasy, having extracted flavor from everything that came before. At this point, it's common to add rice or noodles to the pot, but I prefer to just sip the broth from my bowl. "If you're a real sumo wrestler, are you allowed to just pick up the nabe and slurp the soup right out of it?" I asked.

"If you're a sumo wrestler, you can do whatever you want," replied Iris. "And if someone doesn't like it, squash goes the person."

Later, we came home and turned on the TV. There was a sumo tournament going on in Nagoya, and it played in sports bars across Japan and in our apartment in Nakano. Iris had never seen sumo before, and now she's hooked. I warned her that sumo matches usually last only seconds. She was skeptical. In the very first match we watched, one wrestler charged at the other and fell over. The match was over in *less than half a second*. Actually, what sport could be more perfect for the attention span of a young child?

These days, a lot of sumo wrestlers are Eastern European

bruisers, and at one point we watched an Estonian face off against a Bulgarian. "I'm rooting for the big chubby guy," I told Iris.

"Which one is that?" she asked, then realized she'd been had. We quickly agreed that I would root for the Estonian on the basis of my sliver of Estonian heritage, and she would root for the Bulgarian on the basis that she likes that Bulgarian-style yogurt. It turned out later that the Bulgarian wrestler is actually sponsored by the yogurt brand, and he parades around solemnly in a ceremonial skirt with the Bulgaria Yogurt logo between matches.

I don't remember who won, but I do remember explaining to Iris that if a wrestler's belt falls off, he automatically loses the match.

"I *really* want to see that happen," said Iris.

I *really* don't.

At one point in the history of Japanese food in America, sukiyaki filled the role that sushi plays today as the one Japanese dish that everyone has heard of and which we assume Japanese people eat all the time.

In 1963, Kyu Sakamoto recorded a ballad called, in Japanese, "I Walk Looking Up." He's looking up so people won't see his tears. The physics are debatable, but the melody was universal, and the song became the first Billboard number one hit in a foreign language.

The song, however, wasn't released in the U.S. under its original Japanese title. It was given the Ellis Island treatment, renamed "Sukiyaki" under the assumption that if listeners were familiar with any Japanese word in 1963, it would be this one.

Today, sukiyaki still has a regrettable food–era whiff to it, at least in the U.S., where open-minded eaters gathered for sukiyaki parties before the era of homemade sushi rolls. In Japan, however, sukiyaki is a beloved special-occasion dish. Good sukiyaki restaurants are fancy and expensive. The dish is meant to celebrate the best-quality ingredients, especially beef, and good beef is not cheap. It's easy to spend over $100 per person for sukiyaki, and most restaurants let you choose among multiple grades of beef. The lowest grade will likely be more marbled than anything you've seen before. It's the meat equivalent of the drink sizes at Starbucks: our lowest grade is A+, sir.

Before I say another positive word about sukiyaki, however, I should tell you about what Iris calls the Sukiyaki Disaster.

It was 2010, and Iris and I were in Kyoto. After exploring the geisha district and trying and failing to find the famous stepping stones across the Kamo River, we were ready for something to eat, so we walked into this impossibly skinny alleyway parallel to the river and lined with restaurants and other nightlife. We were confronted immediately by a plastic sukiyaki and *shabu-shabu* display. Shabu-shabu is sukiyaki's ascetic cousin, beef and vegetables cooked in a nearly flavorless broth and dipped in ponzu or another flavorful dipping sauce. The traditional dipping sauce for sukiyaki is...well, I'm getting ahead of myself.

"Sukiyaki?" asked the woman at the counter. "Fifth floor." We went up in a tiny elevator, which let us out into a tatami room overlooking the river. Perfect. We ordered sukiyaki, and the waitress asked if we wanted egg. Sure, I said. The dipping sauce for sukiyaki, you see, is a beaten raw egg. I quite enjoy my sukiyaki this way; you pluck a boiling hot chunk of meat or cabbage or tofu from the bubbling sauce, dunk it briefly in egg, and instantly the food is cool enough to eat and gains the slippery texture of barely-cooked egg. It's like making a runny omelet in miniature with each bite. Japan has no fear of raw eggs, and rice bowl meals are often topped with sweet *donburi* sauce, which is like scrambled eggs seasoned with soy sauce and mirin and pulled from the heat early enough that even a French person would call it undercooked. Once you mix the egg with hot rice, however, wow. I'd better get back to the story.

I expected the waitress to present us each a bowl of egg and let us do the rest. Instead, she cooked all the meat, extracted it from the pot, and divided it between our two bowls of egg, so we each had a pile of delicious beef, completely soaked in raw egg. Iris looked at me as if she'd just seen her favorite stuffed animal set on fire. Now I know what Kyu Sakamoto was crying about. So I gobbled up the sukiyaki, paid the bill, and we went next door to a terrific bar specializing in yakitori. While we ate grilled chicken wings, skewered thigh meat with negi, and shishitō peppers, I promised Iris that we wouldn't go to any more sukiyaki restaurants on that trip. I promised myself that I'd find us a non-catastrophic sukiyaki experience if we ever returned to Japan.

Fast-forward to 2012, to Asakusa Imahan, a 110-year-old sukiyaki restaurant near the restaurant supply district of Kappabashi-dōri. We shucked our shoes and sat in the first floor tatami room. As we got comfortable, our waitress turned our shoes 180 degrees so they'd be in the right orientation to put back on when we left. We ate three tiny, geometrically engineered appetizers, including a perfect cube of kabocha squash-flavored fish cake and an octopus "salad" consisting of one tiny piece of octopus brushed with a plum dressing. Then the waitress uncovered and lit the burner in the center of the table and set a shallow cast-iron pan on top. She poured a thin layer of sauce from a pitcher. Sukiyaki is all about the sauce, a mixture of soy sauce, mirin, sake, and sugar. It is frankly sweet. Usually I'm a tiresome person who complains about overly sweet food, but where soy sauce is involved, I make an exception, because soy sauce and sugar were born to hang.

The waitress set down a platter of thin-sliced Wagyu beef, so marbled that it was nearly white. She asked if we wanted egg. This time I was prepared: only for me, thanks. Then she cooked us each a slice of beef. It was tender enough to cut with your tongue against the roof of your mouth. While we sighed over the meat, she began adding other ingredients to the pan: napa cabbage, tofu, wheat gluten (*fu*), fresh shiitake mushrooms, *shirataki* noodles, chrysanthemum leaves (*shungiku*), and, of course, negi. Suggested tourist slogan: *Tokyo: We put negi in it.*

Then we were left to cook the rest of the meat and vegetables ourselves. I think we nailed it. (Actually, it's impossible to do it wrong.) Like chanko nabe and all Japanese hot pots, sukiyaki gets better as the meal goes on, because the sauce becomes more concentrated and soaks up more flavor from the ingredients cooking in it. At home, Iris and I like to finish off a sukiyaki dinner by ladling the last of the broth into sake cups and toasting with it. If we'd tried this at the restaurant, I imagine it would have produced the world's most uncomfortable nervous laughter, plus the inevitable splash of brown, oily sauce would have required an immediate change of clothes and a long bath.

Which is fine, actually, because Japan is one of the premier places in the world for a bath.

Bathtime

お風呂

IN MY COMMUNITY COLLEGE JAPANESE class, a few months before the trip, we were studying a vocabulary lesson that included the phrase "take a bath," *ofuro ni hairu.* The professor, who grew up in Kyushu, grew wistful. She liked living in Seattle, she said, but could never get used to the inadequate bathtubs.

Bathing in Japan is an obsession. In the days before private bathtubs, people would bathe at the neighborhood *sentō.* These public baths consist of a bathing area separated into male and female baths by a wall inevitably decorated with a mural of Mount Fuji. In all public baths, you must scrub yourself brain-surgeon clean from head to toe at the shower stations before entering the bath to avoid the spread of cooties.

Modern indoor plumbing and prosperity have conspired

to knock off the neighborhood sentō. They still exist but are few in number. We found one in Nakano whose proprietor had posted a handwritten "we're on vacation" sign; it had the look of a failed restaurant sporting the sad delusion, "Remodeling—back soon!"

A bit of the sentō spirit survives in the home bathroom. Believe it or not, it is possible to enforce the "get clean before getting in the tub" rule at home, because Japanese bathrooms have sloping plastic floors with a drain. The idea is to take the handheld shower sprayer to yourself in front of the sink before getting in the deep tub, whose precious hot water can thereby be shared between successive family members. In practice, wow is this problematic, even setting aside the memoir-inducing indignity of being last in line for the lukewarm, cootie-laden tub. I tried prewashing once and couldn't figure out how to avoid spraying water all over the dry towels and other toiletries.

Nowadays, people get their public bathing fix at *onsen* (natural hot springs) and communal baths attached to hotels. Our hotel in Asakusa had a pair of large wooden bathtubs on the top floor that switched genders from time to time so everyone could enjoy the views of Sensō-ji temple and the SkyTree. The water was sometimes pleasant and sometimes hot enough to boil lobsters.

We wanted a quintessential Japanese hot (but not too hot) bath experience. So one day we set out on the Shinkansen bound for Hakone. That's actually an oversimplification. Hakone is a large resort area within the national park that contains Mount Fuji. Getting there and back is more than half the fun. The typical visitor to Hakone travels by *all* of the following modes of transport:

- Shinkansen (or the competing Romance Car train, which is slower but cheaper and with a better name)
- Clickety-clackety mountain train
- Funicular
- Aerial ropeway
- Pirate ship
- Bus

It's not a weekend getaway; it's a Bond film. On the day we went, the aerial ropeway and pirate ships were rained out. We should turn back, I said. Who wants to miss out on pirate ships?

"We're here. Let's check it out," said Laurie. So we got on the Hakone Tozan line, a little red two-car train set that climbs 445 meters up a mountain along tracks lined closely on either side with blooming hydrangeas. Based on the description of the Hakone transport loop and the area's general reputation as an easy tourist destination one hour from Tokyo, I expected Disney-level throngs and gift shops. Not on this rainy day. Like a steep hiking trail, the train tracks zigzagged up the mountain in a series of switchbacks, and at each one, the train came to a stop and the driver walked the length of the car in a formal gait on the way to the booth at the opposite end of the train so we could reverse direction. Whenever the train emerged from a hydrangea corridor, we had a view of the mountain, rimmed with fog.

At the end of the line, the town of Gōra, we ate lunch at a soba place and got on the funicular. I'd never ridden a funicular before and didn't know exactly what it was other than a funny word. A funicular is a slow-moving tram that ascends an incline so steep that the train cars themselves must be built with supports and beams at unconventional angles. If you took a funicular car and put it on flat ground, it would look like it was leaning over.

We chugged up the hill and got off at a random stop because we noticed a billboard advertising a hotel, and nearly every hotel in Hakone has an onsen open to nonguests for a fee. Except for a woman at the front desk, this place was deserted like a horror movie hotel. I asked if we could use the bath, and she said yes, but...hmm... She pulled out a pad of paper and drew a cartoon of raindrops falling into a pool. That's OK, we said. I didn't ask whether the place was haunted or run by the Japanese Norman Bates, but I figure it was one or the other.

The onsen was split into male and female sides, of course, and then subdivided further into indoor and outdoor pools. The outdoor pool, a pastoral composition in concrete and natural stone, was the way to go, a hot bath on a cool day. Yes, we got rained on, which was terrific; they should charge people extra on rainy days. Nobody else was using the onsen, so we could shout back and forth across the corrugated divider. Like, "Hey, Dada, does your indoor pool have a stone bridge!" "Yeah!" "Does your outdoor pool have a big rock in the middle?" "Is your pool haunted?"

(Later, I told my friend Akira about our day in Hakone.

"Did you get rained on in the onsen?" he asked. I said yes. He grinned. "I *love* that!")

On the way back down the mountain, we stopped off at the Hakone Open-Air Museum, a sculpture garden featuring a lot of sculptures you're not allowed to climb and one you are. That one is a massive raindrop of heavy-duty netting called the Woods of Net. Children (adults are, infuriatingly, not allowed) enter through holes in the bottom and get lost inside. Iris spent an hour exploring every cranny of the thing while singing a song that went, "Stuffing kids in a sack / Run away and don't come back."

We got back onto the little mountain train to find an infestation of schoolgirls, dozens of them, in matching uniforms, their heavy leather backpacks monopolizing the luggage racks. Iris could not have been happier if the train had been full of stuffed animals. She planted herself between two girls, and they started playing international hand-slapping games and talking rapidly in Japanese, English, and a hastily-invented pidgin. Twenty minutes later, it was time to say a tearful *sayōnara* with six hundred hugs. I was thinking, *Damn, there are so many of these schoolgirls; would anyone really notice if we brought just two of them home to be Iris's big sisters?*

Later I asked Iris what they had talked about on the train. "You know, what stuff we liked and didn't like," she replied.

"What kind of stuff?"

She shrugged. "The usual stuff. Cats. Airplanes. Snakes."

But you don't have to leave Tokyo to visit a perfectly good onsen. Oedo Onsen Monogatari is an onsen theme park on the island of Odaiba in Tokyo Bay. I realize I've said this over and over again, but if you hear about a destination in Tokyo (other than Tokyo Disney) that sounds like a tourist-clogged disaster area, give it a chance.

Monogatari is an onsen for people who don't want to go far or don't have a lot of onsen experience. It has plenty of English signs and a well-implemented Old Tokyo aesthetic. You sign in at the front desk and choose a *yukata*, a summery cotton kimono, to wear throughout the grounds. All of your worldly possessions and cares go into a locker, and you put on an electronic wristband to keep track of your purchases, which add up quickly. It's like house arrest, with noodles.

Before heading to our respective baths, Laurie, Iris, and I went to the food court and got lunch. I loved this food court, not because the food was especially good (although it was seventeen times better than the average American food court) but because it was such a perfect microcosm of the Japanese dining landscape. There were three noodle stands (udon, soba, and ramen), a sushi stand, a dessert shop selling soft-serve sundaes with fruit jelly and mochi dumplings, and a Korean stand specializing in rice dishes. I went straight for the Korean place and got myself a *dolsot bibimbap,* a hot stone bowl of rice topped with beef, assorted vegetables, and Korean hot sauce. Laurie and Iris returned with ramen and gyōza, and we sat together in the main hall in our yukata.

Because Monogatari draws plenty of international tourists with no prior yukata experience, it's a great place to see yukata wardrobe malfunctions. Inevitably, however, the offenders are more likely to be elderly Belgians than Janet Jackson. I committed a few myself. You're supposed to wear underwear beneath your yukata in the common areas; you're absolutely not allowed to wear anything more than a towel on your head in the sex-segregated bathing areas. If you look up Monogatari online, you will find American tourists complaining about how they didn't realize they would have to get *totally naked* to visit this onsen. And think of the children!

After lunch we went to have our feet nibbled by hundreds of tiny fish. Then, after that—just kidding, I'll explain. The onsen offers a skin treatment where you dip your feet into a shallow pool stocked with *Garra rufa,* also known as doctor fish, which perform primitive exfoliation by slurping dead skin off your feet with their tiny jaws. This is illegal in most U.S. states, where health authorities believe that sharing fish between customers is as sanitary as sharing unsterilized tattoo needles. I find this reasoning persuasive. Naturally, we all went and joined a random stranger at the fish pool.

I'd heard of this fish treatment before, probably from a "hey, you've got to see this" link passed around online, and somehow I had the idea that it involved the occasional wayward fish sidling up to your foot. Try dozens, hundreds, all gnawing simultaneously. You can feel the little bites. At first it provoked an deep-seated piranha fear which I quelled by sitting still, taking deep breaths, and telling myself I had nothing to worry about other than blood-borne diseases. After that, it proved quite relaxing, although I did give up before my allotted fifteen minutes and went back to the painful reflexology pool where you walk around barefoot on jagged rocks. My feet are still baby soft, but when I need my next treatment, I'll post to Craigslist. *Need feet nibbled. Will pay.*

Finally, bathtime. In my view, the purpose of civilization is to avoid wet socks, so I brought along an extra pair in case of locker room puddles. Just before striding naked into the men's bath, I noticed that this was unnecessary. A vending machine sold socks, underwear, toothbrushes, and other locker room essentials. Before getting into the bath proper, I dumped a couple of buckets of hot water over my head from a fountain designed for this purpose. I wondered how many times I'd have to do this before it felt like anything other than the payoff to a slapstick routine.

Monogatari offers a variety of indoor and outdoor pools at different temperatures and with different features, like a whirlpool bath (for some reason, this one was always full of Belgians), a cooling bath, and allegedly beneficial mineral baths, including one called the silk bath where a milky white mineral diffuses softly into the water. I walked to the outdoor area, wrapped my towel around my head, and eased into a stone-lined tub. I closed my eyes, made a beatific face like a Calgon commercial, and immediately confronted the existential challenge of the onsen: to really enjoy it, you have to be surrounded by people you want to talk to or be very comfortable with your own thoughts. I was neither. I tried all the baths in impatient succession and then went and got some vanilla soft-serve with mochi dumplings and hot fudge.

Iris and Laurie, meanwhile, spent the rest of the afternoon lounging in the baths. Afterwards, Laurie deadpanned, "I think the women's baths were probably more aesthetically pleasing than the men's."

"Yeah, I'd have to agree with that," I said. The women's baths, I am told, feature outdoor barrels of water to climb into, big enough for one person or a mother and child. That, and *dozens of naked ladies.*

Dumplings

餃子と小籠包

PAN-FRIED DUMPLINGS HAVE BEEN AMONG Iris's favorite foods since she was less than one year old and I had to chop them into tiny bites so she wouldn't choke on them. A pan-fried dumpling (*gyōza, guo tie,* potsticker, whatever you want to call it) is the most perfect food. At home I fill them with pork and bok choy, ginger and scallions, and assorted seasonings from my Asian sauce collection. My friend Molly once wrote that the inside of my fridge looks like an Asian supermarket; I took this as the highest of compliments.

Back home in Seattle, Iris and I have gone dumpling scouting in restaurants and in our grocer's freezer case. We are not fussy. We had a fling with some Safeway brand dumplings spiked with crunchy lotus root. We often split an order of bargain-basement dumplings at this Sichuan hole in the wall in Seattle's Chinatown, twenty dumplings for $5. Put it in a wrapper and pan-fry it, and I will eat it. Iris feels the same way: she's a green vegetable skeptic ("Actually, I'm an all vegetable skeptic," Iris informed me), but she'll eat her weight in bok choy if it's part of a dumpling.

So it is with a heavy heart that I must report that the dumplings of Tokyo are mostly lousy. I should have known, because Oishinbo devotes a whole episode to the problem, but Yamaoka is a lot pickier than I am about junk food. Here, though, he was right. Unlike cheap noodles, ice cream bars, and convenience-store curry, most gyōza in Tokyo aren't worth eating. The filling tends to be simultaneously bland and too garlicky, and the frying is haphazard.

Any dumplings are better than none, however, and sometimes I ordered a plate of them with my noodles just because I liked having dumplings near me, but eating gyōza in Tokyo mostly provoked in me the most tiresome of food nerd platitudes: *I can make this better at home.* Believe me, I did not say this often in Tokyo. (Iris was kind enough to agree with me about the superiority of my homemade dumplings, but she isn't down on the dumplings of Tokyo the way I am. She's still never met a dumpling she didn't like.)

That's the bad news. The good news is that we found the most ridiculous dumpling experience an hour outside Tokyo and the greatest pan-fried dumplings of our lives ten minutes from our apartment.

In Oishinbo: Ramen and Gyōza, Yamaoka and the gang are on an assignment to help a lonely gyōza chef find a new recipe and true love. While investigating, they have lunch at a dumpling restaurant that boasts "100 types of gyōza" on the sign. (Incidentally, a cute thing about Japanese restaurant chains is that they often put the word "chain" in the name, like, "Gyōza Chain Hanasaki.") They eat dumplings with fillings like garlic-miso, flaked salmon, and Chinese roast pork. Even grumpy Yamaoka had to admit the dumplings were pretty good.

Could such a place be real? Almost. On one boiling hot day, we sat down in a restaurant serving seventy-four types of gyōza, some of which made the fillings mentioned in Oishinbo sound downright normal. The restaurant, however, was not in Tokyo.

Utsunomiya is an ordinary city of half a million, an hour north of Tokyo on the Tōhoku Shinkansen line. It has no particular tourist attractions, and any foreign tourists heading that direction are probably more interested in the beautiful mountain town of Nikko. A few years ago, Utsunomiya's city booster types, as boosters do, went looking around for something about the city to promote. Poring over official statistics, they found that Utsunomiyans eat more gyōza per capita than people of any other city in Japan. "Aha!" said the boosters. "Let it be known far and wide that we are the City of Dumplings."

So, in the early nineties, Utsunomiya went on a gyōza-related development binge. This is not a joke at all. The city boasts a statue of Venus emerging from a gyōza wrapper, which is only *one of many* gyōza-themed statues throughout the downtown area, most of them depicting the dumpling-headed mascot of a particular chain. The dumpling madness begins in the train station, where souvenir shops sell plush stuffed gyōza, frozen gyōza, books about gyōza. A tourist poster plastered everywhere shows thirty-nine of the city's most famous dumplings, crispy-side up. (I especially like the ones where the shaggy crispy layer extends beyond the edge of the dumpling itself, like a skirt.)

There are over two hundred gyōza restaurants in Utsunomiya. I wonder if it's too late to convince the notoriously suggestible Seattle City Council to play catch-up and launch our own gyōza initiative: an exhibit at the Pacific Science Center with a cutaway view of the interior of the gyōza; Pike Place Market fish guys retrained to throw gyōza; and a dumpling eating contest between the two mayors. Our mayor is a big guy, but who knows? Maybe theirs is that little guy who can eat fifty-five hot dogs.

We planned an Utsunomiya gyōza crawl, but when we emerged from the train station into 92-degree weather, we abandoned the idea and just went to the place with (Iris counted) seventy-four types of gyōza, including yogurt, coffee, tea, chocolate, liver, mochi, squid-octopus, sausage, curry, and whale. You can order a whole plate of your favorite variety or a sampler platter; we ordered a sampler (no whale) with a small order of regular pork gyōza as insurance.

The dumplings didn't come with labels, so we were left to guess at their identities. The salted fish roe and curry were easy to pick out, as was the sausage, which had a tiny hot dog inside. After polishing off the sampler, we asked for a plate of yuba gyōza, filled with the tofu skin Iris and I like to make at home. I went spelunking inside the dumplings and found that the pork filling was wrapped in yuba; the snap of fresh yuba was missing, but the dumplings were excellent. I regret not trying the chocolate gyōza. I also regret using the term "delicious membrane."

In one of my favorite books of food essays, *The Importance of Lunch,* John Allemang talks about the day his favorite Greek deli "improved" its baklava with a drizzle of chocolate. Allemang likes chocolate as much as the next guy, but do we have to put in on *everything?*

I thought about this anecdote the first time we ordered lunch at our local soup dumpling restaurant in Nakano. The restaurant, whose name in English is something like "Granddaughter's Shanghai Grilled Soup Dumplings," is a tiny, efficient place which I will call GSD for short.

A soup dumpling is a little marvel of engineering. Called *xiao long bao* in Chinese, *shorompo* in Japanese, and "soupies" by Iris, soup dumplings consist of silky dough wrapped around a minced pork or crab filling. The filling is mixed with chilled gelatinous broth which turns back into soup when the dumplings are steamed. Eating a soup dumpling requires practice. Pop the whole thing in your mouth and fry your tongue; bite it in the wrong place and watch the soup dribble onto your lap.

The reason I thought about chocolate baklava is because GSD pan-fries its soup dumplings. A steamed soup dumpling is perfect just the way it is. Must we pan-fry *everything?*

Based on the available evidence, the answer is yes. Pan-fried soup dumplings are bigger and heartier than the steamed variety and more plump with hot soup. No, that's too understated. I'm exploding with love and soup and I have to tell the world: pan-fried soupies are *amazing*.

The dumplings are served in groups of four, just enough for lunch for one adult or a growing eight-year-old. They're topped with a sprinkle of sesame and scallion. You can mix up a dipping sauce from the dispensers of soy sauce, black vinegar, and chile oil at the table, but I found it unnecessary. Like a slice of pizza, a pan-fried soup dumpling is a complete experience wrapped in dough. Lift a dumpling with your spoon, poke it with a chopstick, press your lips to the puncture wound, and slurp out the soup. (This will come in handy if I'm ever bitten by a soup snake.) No matter how much you extract, there always seems to be a little more broth pooling within as you eat your way through the meaty filling and crispy underside. Then you get to start again, until, too soon, your dumplings are gone.

We never saw anyone working at GSD other than the two women who run the place. At any given time, one is filling the dumplings and the other is minding the purpose-built cast iron griddles. Each griddle's slightly convex top looks like the cooking apparatus at a Mongolian grill restaurant but is recessed into a cylinder and topped with a wooden lid for steaming.

Other customers often ordered a set lunch with dumplings and the rice porridge called congee (*okayu* in Japanese), but we spotted *kyūri* on the giant picture menu on the wall on our first visit, and that became our regular side. One of the proprietors smashed the cucumber to pieces with the dull edge of a cleaver and seasoned it with salt and raw garlic. Later I found a similar recipe in a Fuchsia Dunlop cookbook; she calls it "smacked cucumber," which is exactly it: smacked to order.

Probably I'm harping on this point, but if GSD were transplanted to Seattle, it would land instantly on everybody's ten-best list. In Tokyo, it is merely a neighborhood dumpling restaurant that earns average marks on the online review sites.

Okonomiyaki

お好み焼き

If the waiter offers to prepare your okonomiyaki for
you, take him up on the offer! It's harder than it looks.
—Robb Satterwhite, *What's What in Japanese*
Restaurants

OUR WAITER DID NOT OFFER. But that was OK. I wanted to
go out for okonomiyaki because I figured it would present the
trip's final bout of cultural disorientation, and okonomiyaki
did not disappoint.

The okonomiyaki restaurant we chose was inexplicably
called Penguin Village (in Japanese, *Penginmura*). The exterior featured a gaudy mural of a winking penguin holding
a spatula, welcoming to shore a boat full of dead animals
captained by another (live) penguin. Inside, the guy running
the place was a tall, hunky Japanese surfer dude who looked

like Patrick Swayze in *Point Break*, and the decor consisted of tributes to Japanese professional wrestlers. Japanese professional wrestling combines Hulk Hogan antics with Mexican wrestling masks and, as you might imagine, makes American professional wrestling look like chess.

Okonomiyaki, meanwhile, is to American pancakes what Japanese wrestling is to American wrestling. The basic batter contains flour and water, grated nagaimo (that big slimy yam again), eggs, and diced cabbage. You then augment this base by ordering little bits and nibbles a la carte to be added to the batter. We could not figure out the ordering system, but we listed off ingredients we liked and ended up with two pancakes' worth of batter teeming with squid, octopus, sliced negi, and pickled ginger. The waiter dropped off a big bowl of unmixed pancake fixings and a couple of spatulas and assumed we would know how to do the rest. Every time we did something wrong, he sucked in his breath (a very common sound in Japan, at least in my presence) and intervened. Every time we did something right, he gave the thumbs-up and a Fonzie-like grunt of approval.

Now that I've cooked two okonomiyaki and am certified by the Vera Okonomiyaki Napoletana Association, I can tell you how it's done. If your okonomiyaki has a large featured ingredient like strips of pork belly, set it aside to go on top; don't mix it in. Stir everything else together really well. Pour some oil onto the griddle and smooth it out into a thin film with a spatula. Dump the batter onto the griddle and shape it into a pancake about 1/2 to 3/4 inch thick. If you have pork strips, lay them over the top now like you're making bacon-wrapped meatloaf.

Now wait. And wait. And wait. If little bits of egg seep out around the edge of your pancake, coax them back in. It takes at least five minutes to cook the first side of an okonomiyaki. Maybe ten. Maybe thirty. If you're not hungry enough to drink a tureen of raw batter, it's not ready. Finally, when it's brown on the bottom, slide two spatulas underneath and flip with confidence. Now wait again. When the center is set and the meat is crispy, cut it into wedges and serve with okonomiyaki sauce, mayo, nori, and fish flakes. If you haven't had okonomiyaki sauce, it's a lot like takoyaki sauce. Sorry, just kidding around. It's a lot like tonkatsu sauce.

Iris, who would never eat visible cabbage, raw or cooked, loved everything about Penguin Village and ate four big pancake slices stuffed to the gills with creatures without gills. I wouldn't say okonomiyaki is one of the best things I ate in Japan, but it is a singular experience. If you've never had okonomiyaki, you've never had anything *like* okonomiyaki. It is also dirt-cheap. We went overboard with ordering, and dinner for three was still $15.

Later, an older man came in and stepped behind the counter. He seemed to be Tokyo Swayze's boss. According to Laurie's imagination, the old boss had told Swayze, "I'm leaving you in charge for one hour. Don't worry, it's early. Nobody will come in, and if they do, who cares? They cook all their own food anyway." Then in walk three Americans who've never been to an okonomiyaki place before.

Izakaya Nights

居酒屋

As far as I know, sending someone a free flounder is not a traditional gesture of hospitality in Japan, but that didn't stop the guy two tables over from us at our local izakaya. To explain why a guy sent over a fish at a bar, I need to back up and explain what an izakaya is and why they are so great.

When Iris and I got back from our first trip to Japan, naturally we spent hours telling Laurie about all the places we ate. "There was that bar near the river with the grilled chicken tail," I said.

"And that bar we went to on our last night where I got that ham croquette," added Iris.

We reminisced about several other bars until Laurie said, "Wait, did you really go to a bunch of bars or is this a joke?"

We really went to a bunch of bars. An izakaya is not exactly a bar by American standards; you might say it's the Japanese translation of "gastropub," except that izakaya have been around a lot longer than gastropubs, and the word "gastropub" sounds like a disease, anyway.

In short, an izakaya is a loud, convivial joint serving drinks and a wide assortment of food to go with them. Izakaya are the exception to the rule that the best Japanese restaurants specialize in one type of dish. It's common for an izakaya menu to run a hundred items long.

Take our local izakaya, just down our street, across from Life Supermarket. I will mention the name of the place once, in case you want to look for it: Dainichikarashūzō. Of course, it's written in kanji on the sign, and I'm sorry to report that izakaya are among the toughest restaurants to navigate without Japanese language ability. The menu often consists of a series of painted wooden signs hung on the wall, like the specials you always want to order at a Chinese restaurant.

You can avoid the language barrier by eating at a chain izakaya such as Tsubohachi, which has a picture menu. At any izakaya, however, pointing to the food at neighboring tables is as much of a tradition as sending them a fish, which I'm getting to in a minute.

We'd walked past this place dozens of times already on the way to and from the train station, and it's notable for two things: (1) a comprehensive window display of fish heads and shellfish, including items I'd never seen before, such as pen shell, which looks like a foot-long mussel ("Hey, baby, want to know why they call me Pen Shell?"), and (2) a delicious marine aroma every time the door opens, despite the fact that the place contains dozens of species of fish carcasses. Also, we noticed their morning deliveries from Tsukiji fish market.

So we went to dinner there. I'd been doing pretty well reading Japanese signs and menus and packaging. I felt ready to tackle this izakaya. Well, being able to read the name of an udon shop did not qualify me to distinguish various fish and shellfish species, most of which I wouldn't have recognized if they were written in English. I got so flustered by the menu that I forgot the two most important words in an izakaya: *toriaezu bīru.* "Beer for now."

While I struggled with the menu, a handsome middle-aged guy from a nearby table came over to help. "You like sashimi? Cooked fish? Sushi?" he asked. His English was excellent. He was from originally from Okinawa, he said, and a member of Rotary International. I know nothing about the Rotarians except that it's a service organization; helping befuddled foreigners order food in bars must fall within its definition of charitable service. Our service-oriented neighbor helped us order pressed sweetfish sushi, kisu fish tempura, and butter-sauteed scallops. Dredging up a vague Oishinbo memory, I also ordered broiled sweetfish, a seasonal delicacy said to taste vaguely of melon.

While we started in on our sushi, our waitress—the kind of harried diner waitress who would call customers "hon" in an American restaurant—delivered a huge, beautiful steamed flounder with soy sauce, mirin, and chunks of creamy tofu. "From that guy," she said, indicating the Rotarian samaritan. We retaliated with a large bottle of beer for him and his friend (the friend came over to thank us, with much bowing). What would happen at your neighborhood bar if a couple of confused foreigners came in with a child and didn't even know how to order a drink? Would someone send them a free fish? I should add that it's not exactly common to bring children to an izakaya, but it's not frowned upon, either; also, not every izakaya is equally welcoming. Some, I have heard, are more clubby and are skeptical of nonregulars, whatever their nationality. But I didn't encounter any places like that.

Oh, how was the food? So much of the seafood we eat in the U.S., even in Seattle, is previously frozen, slightly past its prime, or both. All of the seafood at our local izakaya was jump-up-and-bite-you fresh. This was most obvious in the flounder and the scallops. A mild fish, steamed, lightly seasoned, and served with tofu does not sound like a recipe for memorable eating, but it was. The butter-sauteed scallops, meanwhile, would have been at home at a New England seaside shack. They were served with a lettuce and tomato salad and a dollop of mayo. The shellfish were cooked and seasoned perfectly. I've never had a better scallop.

What makes this particular izakaya special is that it's not special. No one would go to Nakano just to eat at this restaurant, because it's surely no better than a fish izakaya in any other neighborhood. These no-name Tokyo holes in the wall could easily go head-to-head with America's top seafood restaurants.

For a deeper dive into izakaya, I met up with Mark Robinson, author of the book *Izakaya*, which looks deceptively like a cookbook, in that it's full of recipes and photos of food. Do not underestimate *Izakaya*. This book, which profiles eight typical Tokyo izakaya, has sucked me in over and over. You will get closer to an izakaya night by reading Mark's book than by visiting any so-called izakaya outside of Japan.

Mark asked me to meet him on Monja Street, on the island of Tsukishima in southeastern Tokyo. *Monjayaki* is Tokyo's homegrown answer to okonomiyaki—a rival pancake, thinner and harder to corral with a spatula—and Monja Street has the highest concentration of monjayaki restaurants in town. We weren't going to any of them. "I hate monja," said Mark. "It's just a big mucusy pancake." With that, we strolled past the Monjayaki Society office, where you can buy a t-shirt featuring a picture of a big mucusy pancake. (I meant to try monjayaki later, because I enjoy eating any food people look down on, but didn't get around to it.)

We walked several blocks down Monja Street, passing about thirty-seven monja restaurants, and finally reached Kishidaya. "I wanted to put this place in the book," said Mark, poking his head underneath the noren and holding up two fingers. "They turned me down. And the hostess is really cute."

Kishidaya is like a mess hall inside, with four long parallel tables and little space in between. The place was packed with happy diners and drinkers, and Mark helped me order a sake. Mark is a handsome half-Japanese guy in his forties, used to easy conversations with cute hostesses.

Japan has a reputation for presenting immigrants with a sturdy glass ceiling; I've had former residents tell me that even after years of living in Japan, they felt like there was always something going on behind their back. You can easily find such tales of woe online: *Japan seemed so great when I visited, and when I moved there, the very polite claws came out.* I asked Mark, who has lived in Tokyo for over twenty years, whether he ever felt this way. "I like being an outsider," he replied. He works as an interpreter for NHK television and gets frustrated by the things that can't be said in official discourse in Japan, things everyone knows are true but would be embarrassing to admit. But outsiders can say whatever they want. A couple of times during the evening, someone asked Mark how long he'd been in Japan, and he clearly enjoyed saying, "Twenty-five years," and also relished surprising people with his fluent Japanese. (I also loved it when someone asked me how long I'd been in Japan. It let me pretend that I spoke better and comported myself with more cultural panache than the average tourist.)

Once the food started arriving, we turned to less weighty topics, like the variety of dishes set in front of us. Unlike our Nakano local, this place wasn't a fish specialist (although they served plenty of good fish), and the food Mark ordered veered toward salty and pickled drinking fare. We had *nuta*, a sweet miso-dressed salad of assorted vegetables including *udo*, the chewy white stem of a mountain plant that should always be referred to by its English name, Japanese spikenard.

Like people everywhere, the Japanese are thrilled when you profess to enjoy their more unusual foods, and my friends Akira and Emi appreciated it when I told them I'd been out for udo and *mozuku*. The latter is a slimy dish of vinegared seaweed which goes especially well with sake. The trick of eating mozuku is to lift just part of the mass of tiny fronds with your chopsticks without picking up the whole thing.

Nobody who saw me eating mozuku would ask how long I'd been in Japan, since the answer was obvious: twelve seconds.

We ate stem ginger, clutching it by the green stalks and dipping the tender rhizomes in miso paste, and *rakkyō*, the Japanese answer to pickled onions, another item to mention if you're trying to portray yourself as an adventurous eater. There was *ohitashi*, blanched spinach marinated in dashi and soy sauce and topped with shaved bonito flakes.

"Is that the famous izakaya tomato?" I asked, pointing to a sign on the wall that simply said "tomato" in katakana. I'd learned about the izakaya tomato from Mark's book; a summer treat, it's just a ripe tomato sliced into wedges and served with salt or mayo or both.

"Yep," said Mark. "Want one?" I'm not usually a big fan of raw tomato, even the good stuff, but when you're sapped by Tokyo's crushing summer humidity, there's nothing better.

As we polished off the tomato, and a beef and tofu stir-fry, and some grilled sardines, I was prepared to say good night and pop back into the subway for the long ride back to Nakano when Mark said, "Are you up for one more place?"

Of course, although I'd finished an entire (small) bottle of sake and my brain felt like a big mucusy pancake. We took a short ride on the Oedo line and surfaced near a sashimi-oriented izakaya called Uoshin. The upstairs counter snaked through the room so everyone could have a seat at the bar, and tucked into nooks at various parts of the arrangement were white-coated chefs, each with a knife and a wooden board full of freshly sliced sashimi. We ordered a few selections from the board, and then Mark, who is apparently one of those wiry guys with a boundless appetite, starting calling for cooked food: *gesoyaki* (grilled squid tentacles, one of my favorites), tamagoyaki (seasoned rolled omelet), and yellow-tail teriyaki, all of which were exceptionally good, especially the meaty broiled yellowtail with its sweet and salty glaze.

That accomplished, Mark made conversation with the two ladies sitting next to us. The younger woman was a local, and her older friend was from out of town, and together they pored over a guide to temples and shrines. I couldn't follow the conversation, but at some point it became clear that the women were saying something to me.

"They're apologizing for the war," explained Mark.

Apology accepted...? The younger woman asked how I was enjoying Japan. I'm the kind of guy who uses the phrase "best thing ever" several times a day, which is not a very Japanese thing to do; presenting an even keel is important, and muted praise is recognized as perhaps more serious than hyperbolic exclamations. (When it comes to expressing abhorrence with a few apparently innocuous words along the lines of, "That's not my favorite," Japanese is unbeatable.)

Noticing a familiar shrine on the cover of their guidebook, however, I thought, *Ah, here is something I can talk about.* "*Fushimi Inari Taisha, desu ne?*" Isn't that the Inari shrine in Kyoto, where Iris and I visited the udon shack?

They didn't know offhand, so they looked it up. Yes, I was right. *So they forced me to keep the guidebook.* I'd violated a key rule of life in Japan: never indicate that you like anything that belongs to someone else, or they will try to give it to you. Once Iris was playing with a friend at a playground and fell in a mud puddle; the friend's mom raced home and returned with a selection of her own daughter's clean clothes, even though we would probably never see them again and would have no way to return the clothes. Laurie managed to wave the gift off, although I'm not sure how.

My bragging about slurping down udo and mozuku must have made an impression on my friend Akira, because a few days later he invited me out for Okinawan food at a restaurant across from Ueno station. Okinawa is a series of tropical islands extending off the tip of Kyushu. It's the host to assorted U.S. military bases, which has had a certain effect on the food. (Everywhere the U.S. Army comes ashore, Spam lands with it.) Tokyo has it bad for Okinawan food and culture, which I think has a lot to do with hardworking people wishing they were on island time. If you can't make it all the way to Hawaii, Okinawa will do. One weekend, Nakano was overtaken by an Okinawan cultural festival with much dancing and drumming. Akira, who is not Okinawan, is a member of an Okinawan dance troupe. And then there was dinner.

Okinawan food is completely different from...well, I was about to say "mainland food," as if any part of Japan could be considered mainland. Anyone who finds Japanese food challenging will be alternately reassured and driven to drink by Okinawan food, which is good, because we drank a lot. "What are you drinking?" I asked.

"Beer," replied Akira. "Always beer."

We ordered many highlights of Okinawan cuisine, including its best-known dish, *goya champuru,* bitter melon stir-fried with pork and tofu. Bitter melon is bitter the way Peeps are sweet: overpoweringly so. I like it. We ate *umi budō,* or "sea grapes," which look like those fancy little "champagne grapes" but are actually a seaweed; the translucent orbs pop in your mouth like caviar. Okinawa consumes sea vegetables to a degree that makes the rest of Japan look seaweed-phobic. In addition to the sea grapes, we had more mozuku, this time fried up as tempura, a shaggy mass of greenery in a light crust.

Soon we were joined by Akira's friends Riku ("call me Rikuchan") and Eddie, who tested my Japanese skills further. Akira speaks very good English but did a good job of playing language cop when I got tired of speaking Japanese and tried to slide back into my native tongue. "*Gambatte,* Matthew-san!" he would say. You can do it! I managed to divine that Riku had once been to Seattle and that quiet Eddie plays guitar in a band with Akira. I think the explanation involved more air guitar than spoken language, however.

We ordered more food, including pasta salad and curly fries with ketchup, but also *pō-pō,* a rolled crepe spread with miso and ground meat, which I loved. My language skills were not helped along when we switched from beer to *awamori,* Okinawan whiskey. Several times I made it ten words deep into a subordinate clause before abandoning the whole sentence like a sinking ship.

My only complaint about izakaya nights can be summed up in one word: smoke. Seattle banned smoking in bars and restaurants years ago, and to be confronted by a cloud of cigarette smoke in an otherwise welcoming restaurant felt like a betrayal, a literally smoking fissure in the fabric of civilization. But I had no reason to feel superior, because most of Tokyo has banned smoking *on the street.*

The Takoyaki Chronicles

たこ焼き

Y<small>OYOGI</small> P<small>ARK</small>, <small>IN</small> H<small>ARAJUKU</small>, <small>IS</small> best known for its gaggles of bizarrely clad fashionistas who congregate there on Sundays. We went one rainy Sunday and saw no gothic Lolitas or other rare species; a cafe employee said the rain had likely scared them off, but apparently the weekly parade has been growing sparse even on sunny days. Either that or the latest cosplay style is to dress up as trees, Macbeth-style.

We did, however, find a wishing tree for *tanabata*. Tanabata is a summer festival during which, among other things, people write their wishes on strips of paper and tie them to a bamboo tree. Then, in August, Santa comes and…wait, wrong tradition.

Iris, not usually known for practical wishes (she seems to actually believe that a trillion dollars is something she might stumble into), wrote "Iris loves takoyaki" on her paper, and her wish came true again and again.

I

Takoyaki are octopus balls—not, thankfully, in the anatomical sense. They're a spherical cake with a chunk of boiled octopus in the center, cooked on a special griddle with hemispherical indentations. If you're familiar with the Danish pancakes called *aebleskivers,* you know what a takoyaki looks like; the pan is also similar.

Takoyaki are not unknown in the U.S., but I've only ever seen them made fresh at cultural festivals. Iris is a big fan, but I've always been more into the takoyaki aesthetic than the actual food. Takoyaki are always served in a paper or wooden boat and usually topped with mayonnaise, bonito flakes, shredded nori, and takoyaki sauce.

The presentation is terrific. Iris and I once spent several days painstakingly assembling a model takoyaki stand a friend bought for us at a Japanese imports store. We rolled modeling clay into takoyaki balls and basted them with brown paint, folded tiny paper boats, and even sculpted a fake cast-iron takoyaki pan. When people come to visit, Iris proudly leads them to the bookshelf and says, "We built this takoyaki stand!"

"That's great," says the guest. "What's a takoyaki stand?"

This never gets old, nor do I ever tire of watching people blanch when I throw the phrase "octopus balls" into a conversation. The takoyaki ball itself, however, whether freshly made or bought in the Uwajimaya freezer case and nuked, is just a mushy dough ball with a tiny, chewy nub of tasteless mollusk inside.

Or so I thought.

II

Remember all the way back at the beginning when we walked from Nakano Station into the Sun Mall and turned right at Gindaco? This time, let's stop for lunch.

Gindaco is a chain restaurant, so you can also find it in plenty of other places in Tokyo. (Oddly, it's one of the few restaurants in Japan with many drive-through locations, though not in central Tokyo. Given that the food is hot, saucy balls of dough, this seems as safe as a drive-through knife shop.)

When you visit Gindaco, spend some time watching the cooks make takoyaki before ordering, because it's an amazing free show. The shop has an industrial-sized takoyaki griddle with dozens of hot cast iron wells, each one about an inch and a half in diameter. The cook squirts the grill with plenty of vegetable oil. She dunks a pitcher into a barrel of pancake batter and sloshes it over the grill, then strews the whole area with negi, ginger, and huge, tender octopus chunks. Some of Gindaco's purple tentacles are two inches long. This cooks for a little while, then the cook tops off the grill with more batter until it's nearly full.

Up to this point, the process looks haphazard, but then she whips out the skewers. Using only the same slender bamboo skewers you'd use for making kebabs, she begins slicing through the batter in a grid pattern and forming a ball in each well. Somehow she herds this ocean of batter into a grid of takoyaki in a minute or two.

The takoyaki cost all of 500 yen, and the price includes a wooden serving boat that you can take home and reuse as a bath toy if you haven't gotten too much sauce on it. A Ginda-co takoyaki is a brilliant morsel: full of flavor from the negi and ginger, crispy on the outside and juicy within. Takoyaki also stay mouth-searingly hot inside for longer than you can stand to wait, so be careful.

III

We spent a day on Odaiba, an artificial island in Tokyo Bay. Odaiba is one of my least favorite places in Tokyo. Grumpy dad alert: it's far from everything and it's mostly a collection of shopping malls.

Iris loves Odaiba. We went there do to a few of her favorite things: ride a Ferris wheel (I'm afraid of heights), ride around in self-driving Toyotas (I prefer trains), and go to a mall which replicated old Hong Kong and featured two floors of Chinese restaurants (now we are speaking my language). Unfortunately for me, the Chinese-themed mall had shut down. Damn you, Odaiba! Fortunately for Iris, the Chinese area had been replaced with Legoland. Iris and I hung out at Legoland for a couple of hours, admiring the Lego repli-ca of Tokyo, complete with a ten-foot-tall SkyTree, Sensō-ji temple, and moving trains. We stuck around long enough for Iris to forget about the Ferris wheel, and then we looked for something to eat. That's when we stumbled on the Odaiba Takoyaki Museum.

As you enter the takoyaki museum, you're greeted by a giant model takoyaki boat piloted by a cute takoyaki with arms and legs. Human legs, not octopus legs. The takoyaki museum is not a museum; it's a food court populated entirely by takoyaki restaurants from all over Japan. Tokyo boasts similar food theme parks devoted to ramen, gyōza, ice cream, and desserts. If you don't like takoyaki, you're not entirely out of luck: the stand we visited, Aizuya, also offers *radioyaki*. You would think radioyaki would mean "takoyaki that grows arms and legs after exposure to nuclear radiation," but no, it replaces the octopus with *konnyaku* and beef gristle. Konnyaku is a noncaloric gelatin made from the root of a plant closely related to the stinking corpseflower.

On the counter at Aizuya, they'd put out a copy of Oishinbo featuring their restaurant, which was one of the earliest takoyaki places in Osaka. Aizuya serves only naked takoyaki, without toppings, which made Iris very happy because she is eight and suspicious of all condiments. I did my best to make conversation with the countermen. "Oishinbo!" I said. "I like Oishinbo. I read it at home. I like takoyaki." That was as far as I got. Luckily, by then the takoyaki were ready. We ate them next to a wall mural depicting the Odaiba Ferris wheel with takoyaki instead of ride cars. The takoyaki were...well, I still preferred Gindaco. (I definitely recommend the chewy radioyaki, even if you don't think you're a fan of beef gristle and corpseflower starch.)

The fact that my favorite takoyaki come from a chain

restaurant probably says a lot about my plebeian tastes. Still, the takoyaki museum is one of my favorite places in Tokyo, for two reasons. First, it sent Laurie into an existential haze. She kept looking around and saying, "I can't believe we're in a takoyaki museum." In Seattle, takoyaki are some weird food that Iris and I discovered deep in the freezer case at Uwajimaya. In Tokyo, there is a whole theme park devoted to them.

Second, the takoyaki museum has the greatest gift shop in the world. Whenever I take Iris to a tourist attraction, I'm always looking ahead for an excuse to bypass the gift shop. "If we skip the gift shop, we'll have time for ice cream." That sort of thing. I would skip ice cream to shop at the takoyaki museum gift shop, which is almost entirely octopus-themed. They sell not only cute plush stuffed octopuses, but also *cute plush stuffed takoyaki.* We bought Iris a smiling takoyaki coin purse, and she bought herself a cute little red octopus. She named it Tako, and it lives in her bed. You can buy takoyaki postcards, takoyaki-flavored snack foods, and tell-all takoyaki chef memoirs. I made up the last part, but who knows? I did not make up the coin-operated takoyaki carnival video games, of which there were two: Takoyaki Heroes and Takoyaki Sniper.

There are still five takoyaki places at the museum I haven't tried, so I'm ready to head back to Odaiba any time.

IV

We signed up for a home visit with a Tokyo family through a company called Nagomi Kitchen. For a nominal fee, we'd get to visit an average Japanese family at their house for lunch. We requested a family with kids, and the agency matched us with the Usui family of Saitama prefecture.

"Have you tried takoyaki?" asked mom Kanae Usui when we got to their house.

"I LOVE takoyaki," replied Iris. The family's takoyaki grill was sitting, ready for action, on a kid-sized table. Kanae took the batter and a tray of octopus chunks out of the fridge and put the kids to work. Much of the cooking, and this is no exaggeration, was done by Nao Usui, age 2. She stood authoritatively at the head of the takoyaki griddle with her skewers, distributing octopus and coaxing the batter into balls exactly like they do at Gindaco. I've been a food writer for over ten years and have watched countless hours of Food Network and dozens of chefs doing their thing live, and I have never seen a feat of cooking as impressive as Nao Usui making takoyaki. I took a bunch of photos, and she shot me a look to say, "Hey, dumbass, how do you expect me to do my job while holding up the peace sign, as required in all photos by Japanese law?" The takoyaki were much better than the ones at the museum, although I would say that about anything cooked by Nao Usui.

V

Our final takoyaki surprise happened at Mister Donut.

They don't make an octopus doughnut at Mister Donut, although it wouldn't be any weirder than their Double Kare-pan, a stick of pink fried dough with two pockets of curry inside, each a different flavor. (It's not bad at all.) What they do make is doughnut holes served in a paper takoyaki boat. When Iris saw this, she devised a complex system of justice for anyone who passed Mister Donut and witnessed the takoyaki doughnut holes without buying them, or—worse—eating them without bringing home Iris's fair share. All of the punishments under this system, coincidentally, involved giving Iris extra doughnuts. This is probably one of the early signs your kid will be getting an MBA.

Just an American Girl Eating Tokyo Sweets

洋菓子

Tom Cavanagh: *How does a chocolate bar that looks exactly like a Kit Kat taste completely like melon?*

Michael Ian Black: *They can do anything in Japan.*
—*Mike and Tom Eat Snacks*

TOKYO IS A CITY OF sweets, and there is a Berlin Wall down the middle of its sweet tooth, separating traditional Japanese confections (*wagashi*) from Western ones (*yōgashi*). Wagashi are high art, the zenith of Japan's obsession with presentation, packaging, wordplay, and gift-giving, and the ultimate test of a foreigner's tolerance for bean paste. Wagashi shops look like jewelry stores or museum cases, displaying perfect little seasonal confections under glass. The candies themselves, often meant to be eaten with matcha as part of the tea ceremony, are—to radically oversimplify the incredibly diverse world of wagashi—most commonly fusions of mochi, red and white bean paste, and fruits, and sometimes vegetables, herbs, syrups, and other flavorings. In size and shape, wagashi resemble the offerings at European chocolate shops; in color and flavor, not so much.

To anyone who grew up with beans on the savory side of the plate, the Japanese way with bean paste is a hard sell. I know plenty of Westerners who've developed an appreciation for the stuff, and I feel provincial not to be able to count myself among them, but the smooth, reddish paste of sweetened, mashed adzuki beans is just too much like the contents of a bean burrito. (My friend Rachael has lived in Japan several times and reports that it took her six years to begin appreciating the stuff.) You'll see white bean paste, which tastes similar, and green bean paste, which is made from mashed edamame. The green paste is my favorite, since I love edamame, and eating it wrapped in mochi isn't too much of a stretch.

Tales of wagashi gave Laurie bad premonitions: she has a powerful sweet tooth and a fear of bean paste. Luckily, Japan is known for reverse engineering Western inventions and perfecting them, and nowhere is this done to more delicious effect than in the world of desserts.

What is the cure for 90-degree weather that settles on you like a sweaty Sasquatch by 10 a.m.? In two words, ice cream. We ate so much ice cream, it's a wonder we didn't start playing "Turkey in the Straw" when we walked around. Baskin-Robbins has shops all over Tokyo, and they feature some local flavors like green tea and Popping Shower, studded with Pop

Rocks. We stopped in at Baskin-Robbins near the beginning of July and sat across from a poster of a three-scoop cone with the slogan CHALLENGE THE TRIPLE. This became something of a rallying cry. If you're not seizing the opportunities presented by life in Tokyo or life in general, you're not challenging the triple. And the best place to challenge the metaphorical triple is at Dairy Chiko.

Dairy Chiko, in the basement of Nakano Broadway, is a surrealist ice cream shop known for octuple-decker soft-serve cones. You can also order a smaller cone with less than one billion calories, but the draw at Dairy Chiko is watching how other people eat their towering cones of vanilla, yuzu, milk tea, matcha, ramune, orange, strawberry, and chocolate (flavors may vary). Walking while eating is taboo in Japan, and Dairy Chiko has no seating area, so people loiter near the stand, two to a cone, drawing spoons up the sides of the ice cream, trying to forestall the inevitable. Old ladies, meanwhile, usually order a small matcha cone and eat it with a spoon, avoiding the shame of a green milk mustache. Near Dairy Chiko is a cafe with a public seating area and a very angry-looking drawing of an eight-layer cone with the international NO symbol superimposed on it.

Soft-serve ice cream, called "soft cream," is much more popular in Tokyo than hard ice cream. I've always been something of a soft cream partisan and consider the Dairy Queen Peanut Buster Parfait a perfect dish. In Tokyo, you can find soft ice cream made with the finest ingredients, as at the Ladurée Soft Cream stand at Shinjuku station, where I had probably the best chocolate ice cream of my life and where

Laurie paid over $1 for a topping of two fresh raspberries. Outside a public park one day, a cafe stand did a brisk business selling iced coffee and tea and cones of soy milk (*tōnyu*) soft cream. My friend Akira shared a bite with me, and as the smooth, earthy stuff melted on my tongue, I thought about the ignominious fate of soy milk in America. Until recently, I knew soy milk only as that stuff in the aseptic carton that ruins the lattes of the lactose-intolerant; real soy milk is something different, and a real soy ice cream cone is pure pleasure.

Ice cream lovers in Tokyo spend a lot of time with their heads in convenience store freezer cases. The most obvious difference between Japanese and American ice cream bars is that if the Japanese bar promises something crispy, it will damn well be crispy. The Haagen-Dazs Crispy Sandwich, for example, is a slim bar of ice cream between two delicate wafers. How do they keep the wafers from getting soggy? Is it a layer of shellac? Maybe it's best not to ask. Crepes, soft but not mushy, are also a frequent player in ice cream bars.

Near the end of the month I discovered my single favorite ice cream treat, the Black Thunder bar, a chocolate ice cream bar on a stick filled with crunchy chocolate cookie chunks. I also tried its sister product, the vanilla White Thunder, but in the immortal words of Wesley Snipes: *always bet on Black Thunder.*

Iris and I also became mildly obsessed with Zachrich, a triangular Choco Taco–like bar that looked like a run-over sugar cone, coated with chocolate on the inside and filled with mint ice cream. And Iris often selected Coolish, a foil canteen of soft-serve that you warm with your hands until it's just melted enough to suck out through the spout. (All of these names, incidentally, are in English; I'm not translating them.)

If I'm making it sound like we went around eating dessert all the time, it's because we went around eating dessert all the time. That's why they call it vacation. A day that ended with Black Thunder probably began with a trip to Mister Donut.

The story of Mister Donut begins in the U.S., where it was a Dunkin' Donuts competitor in the 1950s. The American division was eventually acquired by Dunkin', but the chain still thrives in Japan and is now as Japanese as Yoshinoya or Hanamaru Udon. (There is exactly one Mister Donut remaining in the U.S., in suburban St. Louis.) Most of the doughnuts will be familiar to Western eyes, but the signature Pon de Ring gets its chewy texture from mochi; matcha doughnuts are always available; and they've occasionally offered a jelly doughnut filled with red bean paste.

On our first trip to Japan, I promised Iris that when we returned, we'd sign up for a Mister Donut point card and earn a prize. This turned out to be a snap. When we'd racked up 100 points (this was not hard to do; in addition to the doughnuts, the iced coffee at Mister Donut is superb), Iris perused the prize chart and selected a tenugui imprinted with Pon de Lion, Mister Donut's mascot, whose mane is a Pon de Ring doughnut.

Mister Donut is where I felt most keenly the otherworldly charm of Tokyo customer service. Every time we went to their Nakano location, around the corner from the entrance to Nakano Broadway, the staff treated us like Beyoncé, Jay-Z, and Blue Ivy. The body language, the facial expressions, the mechanics of the transaction—all of it said, *You are our favorite customers, and we're so lucky to have you in our humble doughnut shop.* This service ethic wasn't unique to Mister Donut by any means, and it had nothing to do with the fact that we were obvious foreigners. We encountered the same level of service at department stores, bakeries, fast food restaurants, bookstores, and the post office. It never seemed fake or obsequious. If Tokyo's service employees are faking it, they're doing it so well that they're probably fooling themselves, too. Bad service in Tokyo is shockingly rare, and being able to walk into any shop and be treated like a human made me realize how painful it is when you can't depend on such treatment. Don't get me wrong; it's equally painful to hear people complain about bad service online.

Japan is obsessed with French pastry. Yes, I know everyone who has access to French pastry is obsessed with it, but in Tokyo they've taken it to another level. When a patissier becomes sufficiently famous in Paris, they open a shop in Tokyo; the department store food halls feature Pierre Herme, Henri Charpentier, and Sadaharu Aoki, who was born in Tokyo but became famous for his Japanese-influenced pastries in Paris before opening shops in his hometown. And don't forget the famous Monsieur Donut, which I just made up.

Our favorite French pastry shop is run by a Japanese chef, Terai Norihiko, who studied in France and Belgium and opened a small shop called Aigre-Douce, in the Mejiro neighborhood. Aigre-Douce is a pastry museum, the kind of place where everything looks too beautiful to eat. On her first couple of visits, Iris chose a gooey caramel brownie concoction, but she and Laurie soon sparred over the affections of Wallace, a round two-layer cake with lime cream atop chocolate, separated by a paper-thin square chocolate wafer. "Wallace is a one-woman man," said Laurie.

Iris giggled in the way eight-year-olds do at anything that smacks of romance. We never figured out why they named a cake Wallace. I blame IKEA. I've always been more interested in chocolate than fruit desserts, but for some reason, perhaps because it was summer and the fruit desserts looked so good and I was not quite myself the whole month, I gravitated toward the blackberry and raspberry items, like a cup of raspberry puree with chantilly cream and a layer of sponge cake.

One of the joys of eating French pastry in Tokyo is availing yourself of French dessert artistry with a Japanese standard of customer service. When you ask for a cake to go on a hot day, they'll ask how soon you intend to eat it, and then pack it for travel with tiny ice packs taped to the inside of the box for temperature control and protection against bumps and bruises. We collected a bunch of these ice packs and occasionally brought them out of the freezer to apply to our foreheads when we got home from running sweaty errands.

The opposite of Aigre-Douce is Sweets Forest, a dessert theme park in the trendy Jiyūgaoka neighborhood in southwest Tokyo. Sweets Forest has no French restraint; it's worth visiting not so much for the sweets but because it is an only-in-Tokyo experience. The place is done up like a fairytale forest punctuated with dessert counters and seating areas. Iris immediately chose an ice cream counter called (really) Mix n' Mixream, which was like Cold Stone Creamery only good, and asked the guy to bash sponge cake, coconut, and other assorted solids into her ice cream.

Meanwhile, I went to a place specializing in sponge cake roulades in dozens of flavors. (Sponge cake, pudding, and flan are especially popular in Tokyo and keep showing up in contexts expected and otherwise.) I selected two tiny cakes, one black sesame and one whose flavor I never quite figured out, but soybeans were definitely involved. Banners at Sweets Forest announced a Princess Jiyūgaoka Sweets pageant that Iris desperately wanted to enter, although I think the contest was for desserts, not people. Then, while Laurie ate a strawberry sundae from Berry Berry (everything on the menu is strawberry), Iris led me to a *gachapon* machine. Gachapon are vending machines that sell cheap toys in plastic capsules; sadly, the merchandise is usually as crappy as you'd find in any other country, but this time Iris scored a keychain adorned with the figurine of an anime character with the greatest name ever: Easter Chopperman.

One of the best desserts we had in Tokyo, however, was at Denny's. One hot afternoon in Asakusa, Iris and I split the Devil's Sundae, a towering assemblage of chocolate and vanilla ice cream, a slug of jellied chocolate pudding, Cocoa Puffs, banana slices, chocolate syrup, and whipped cream. This is not, by a long shot, the most absurd sundae you can get in Tokyo. We saw ads for a SkyTree sundae, 63.4 centimeters tall (exactly 1/1000th the height of the real SkyTree) and topped with a crown of whipped cream taller than some children.

Tokyo supermarkets, like American ones, have a well-stocked yogurt section. Unlike in America, however, the popularity of yogurt extends to the candy section. I've long been a fan of Hi-Chew, the Japanese fruit chews, for their resilient texture and uncannily accurate fruit flavors: sour cherry, apple, grape, pickled plum, and especially mango, which is closer to the flavor of an actual tropical mango than most imported mangoes.

Only in Tokyo, however, have I seen yogurt Hi-Chew, whose pure white candy cubes taste exactly like good plain yogurt. Bulgaria brand yogurt, makers of the drinkable yogurt that ruined Laurie's tea, offers a competing candy which is more like yogurt-flavored Mentos. Bulgaria: the fermentedmaker! We brought home several packages of yogurt Hi-Chew; only one remains, and I'm looking at it lustfully right now.

Finally, let's talk about those Kit Kat bars. There is no flavor that cannot be embodied in Kit Kat form and sold in Japanese stores. Green tea. Black tea. Miso. Cherry blossom. Soy sauce. Toasted soybean powder (*kinako*). Chile. Orange. Melon. Only a few are available at any given time, and right now, evil geniuses at Nestlé are coming up with new flavors. I'd like to suggest okonomiyaki flavor, which would consist of a bag of assorted flavors (ginger, squid, mountain yam, egg) that could be combined in the proportions of your choice, just like a real okonomiyaki. Sauce and Kewpie mayo optional.

We bought a SkyTree orange Kit Kat, which was a regular orange Kit Kat in a preposterously long box, and the Yubari melon Kit Kat, which tasted exactly like melon, was sold in a fancy gift box, and cost $200. Two-thirds of that is true.

Note: *On their respective corporate websites, you can find the compete illustrated history of Hi-Chew and Mister Donut, including every flavor/style ever offered and the date of its debut, going back to the 1970s. See http://www.morinaga.co.jp/hi-chew/history/index.html and http://www.misterdonut.jp/museum/donut/y2013.html.*

Warning: *This is more addictive than any YouTube channel.*

Additional warning: *These sites are in Japanese, but like other websites you may be familiar with, if you can't read the language, you'll have plenty of fun clicking around and looking at the pictures.*

Eel

うなぎ

JUST EAST OF THE GREEN banner marking the entrance to Pretty Good #1 Alley in Nakano, an old man drives a spike into the head of an eel every morning at 9 a.m. He then inserts the tip of his specialized eel knife behind the collarbone and, with the musical rattle of metal on bone, butterflies the fish and removes its backbone.

This is his first eel of the day. He cuts the fillet into four-inch strips and threads them onto skewers. Once the prep is done, he fires up the grill with *binchotan*, an expensive type of clean-burning hardwood charcoal. In Tokyo, "fanning the flames" isn't just an expression. It's an actual cooking method, and you can walk past the eel stand any time of the afternoon and get hit with a blast of heat and the aroma of charcoal-grilled eel.

Summer is the time to eat eel in Japan. Even Yoshinoya,

the beef-bowl chain, offers an eel bowl special, which sounds as promising as a McDonald's sea urchin special. On the Day of the Ox, in late July or early August, people all over Japan line up to eat eel. If you eat eel on this sweltering day, it is said, you will be fortified with the stamina to survive the rest of the disgusting Japanese summer. Why eel and not, say, ox? I bet it's a penis thing.

Eel, at least the freshwater eel called unagi, was not having a great summer when we were there. True, any summer in which someone drives a spike into your head is pretty lousy, but unagi has been on the Seafood Watch red list for years, and in 2012 prices skyrocketed, indicating dwindling supply. This is bad. Eels have a complex lifecycle that makes them vulnerable to overfishing. Also, they are kind of dumb and easy to scoop out of rivers in mass quantities. Worse yet, they're ugly; it's harder to drum up sympathy for a slimy, snakelike fish than for a majestic whale. Finally, when prepared well, eels are among the most delicious of all fish. They offer the earthiness of catfish; a firm but yielding texture; slippery, edible skin; and the delightful crunch of tiny pin bones. It is hard to make eel sound tasty to someone who hasn't tried it, but isn't the same true of oysters, beef tongue, or plenty of smelly and gooey tropical fruits?

So why did I eat it? It was there, it was delicious, and everyone else was eating it. Do I care about sustainability issues? Yes. Did I care enough that I was able to resist the temptation to eat this delicious, endangered fish? No.

Iris and I went to the eel restaurant in early July, just the two of us. We ordered the only thing on the menu, *unaju,* barbecued eel fillet on rice in a lacquer box. There was a young guy working alongside the old man, and he wanted to make sure we understood that each serving was 1800 yen, or about $23. (See? Expensive.) The old man waved his hand at this and said something like, "Let them order their food in peace." He reheated two skewers of eel fillets over the fire, brushed them with sauce, and then removed the bamboo skewers by twisting each one smartly before sliding it out. The younger guy placed the eel meat atop our rice and then pulled out the world's coolest cooking utensil. My jaw literally dropped. I looked over at Iris. Her mouth was hanging open, too. The world's coolest cooking utensil is a sauce ladle. The cup at the end of the handle is a cube with three thin spouts emerging from the side, better to dispense sauce thinly over a wide area. It's a tiny watering can for sauce—in this case, sweet eel sauce, made from eel bone broth enriched with soy sauce, sugar, and mirin.

Iris and I finished every bite of our eel and rice, paid our $46, and then ran home to tell Laurie about the amazing sauce ladle. Later, I found the ladle for sale at the big DIY store Tokyu Hands (suggested motto: "Get Handsy!"), earning several minutes of hero worship from Iris.

In the days leading up to the Day of the Ox, our local eel place posted a sign inviting people to preorder their eel or, presumably, risk spending the remainder of the summer in a lugubrious pallor. I thought about preordering but decided it would overtax my fragile language abilities, so instead I just sent a cute kid to go buy our eel on the day itself.

Iris headed down the street, her takoyaki coin purse

swinging around her neck. She was gone for a long time. Finally, she returned with a beautifully wrapped package. "I made some new friends at the eel place," she reported. Apparently, eight-year-old American girls don't come in to buy eel every day. The package contained two eel skewers and two tiny red-capped bottles of eel sauce. I heated the fillets in the toaster oven. Removing the skewers was not nearly as easy as the eel guy had made it look, but eventually I gave it the right dose of elbow grease and placed the eel over rice. Iris poured the sauce into the world's coolest cooking utensil and sauced our *unadon,* which is what you call eel on rice when it's not served in a fancy box. It was the perfect lunch, and I can report conclusively that my stamina never flagged for the rest of the summer, except on days of muggy, 88-degree heat—that is, every day.

After the Day of the Ox, every time we walked past the eel place, anyone working there waved and shouted, "Iris!" I realize this is the kind of hey-look-at-us story that sends real travel writers into a lugubrious pallor, but come on, it was great.

In Oishinbo: Izakaya Pub Food, an American reporter wants to impress his boss with his knowledge of Japanese cuisine, so Yamaoka and Kurita take the visiting foreigners to a skewer restaurant in Nakano.

"You must make great yakitori," says the American boss.

The chef looks stricken. "We don't do yakitori," he replies, indicating an anatomical wall chart of the Japanese eel, *Anguilla japonica.* The chef then grills up ten different skewers of eel, including the spine, the liver, the fin, and the guts. (How you get fish guts to stay on a skewer, I do not know.)

Before the trip, I went onto Flickr to look at pictures of Nakano, and I recognized a frame from this Oishinbo book stuck on the window of a building. *That's odd,* I thought. *Maybe they sell manga. Or maybe some Oishinbo fan went crazy with wheat paste and started posting bills.*

It took far too long for me to come to the following realizations:

- The building didn't look like a comic shop.
- In fact, it looked more like a restaurant.

This prompted two questions:

- Wait, could the place in the book be based on an actual restaurant?
- Am I looking at the ten-skewers-of-eel restaurant?

I found the answers on Tabelog.com, Japan's answer to Yelp: yes and (fist pump) yes! The restaurant is called Kawajirō, and it's a seven-minute walk from our apartment, in a tiny Mediterranean-style public square just east of the entrance to Nakano Broadway mall.

Kawajirō is a tiny restaurant, one of the most popular places in Nakano, and the most highly rated on Tabelog. It's the only restaurant in Nakano where we ever saw people line up. The first time we tried to go there, we failed. We showed up around 6 p.m. and got in line. By 7:30, the line hadn't moved at all, and so we left and got tempura instead.

Between 6:00 and 7:30, however…

There is a soba noodle shop whose kitchen opens onto the same courtyard as the front door of Kawajirō. The soba chef, tall, bald, and wrinkled, glowered in the doorway, staring at the line of people waiting to get into his rival. His stare was so intense, it was like he was just trying to make us burst into flames. I never saw anybody go into the soba place.

Meanwhile, an old man rode up on a bicycle. People in Tokyo use their bicycles to lug all sorts of parcels: multiple children, groceries, home improvement supplies, and so on. This guy had something on the back of his bike covered by a large sheet of burlap. A saw hung precariously off the side of the bike. The man hopped off his bike and pulled aside the burlap to reveal a large chunk of ice. He sawed off a large brick and carried it into another restaurant, then returned, secured his load, and rode off. In retrospect, I can't believe we didn't go to *that* restaurant. If Portland hipsters aren't making artisan ice deliveries yet, what is wrong with them?

The following night, we lined up thirty minutes before Kawajirō opened. The soba chef was there again, doing his thing. Possibly he died years ago, penniless, and his angry ghost shows up every night looking for revenge.

Finally, we stepped through the bead curtain for the first seating at the bar. (The place is all bar except for one table crammed into the back, and what seemed to be a private upstairs room.) I was nervous about how to order, since I have no idea what the parts of the eel are called in Japanese, but everyone was ordering the set menu, with six assorted skewers, and we did the same. The extremely handsome chef stood at the front of the restaurant tending the grill. He wore a summery but tailored blue button-down and seemed impossible to ruffle, like President Obama. Whenever he needed to salt the food, he held a fistful of loaded-up skewers over the floor and scattered them with sea salt, and as he finished each batch of skewers, he dipped them in sauce and dealt them out to diners like cards.

We ate spiral-wrapped eel meat. We ate guts. We ate liver, which is somehow different from guts. We (mostly Iris) ate two bowls of crispy fried eel backbones. We ate eel meat wrapped around burdock root and eel fin wrapped around garlic chives. We ate smoked eel that tasted like Jewish deli food. I ate better than anyone, because I was the only member of the family willing to try the offal. All of it was precisely like Oishinbo, down to the eel anatomy chart on the wall. It was like stepping into a book, *Neverending Story*–style, and isn't a Luck Dragon just a big furry eel?

At the end of the meal, we handed over some cash, and the woman behind the counter pulled down a DuckTales cookie can and fished around in it for our change.

Later that night, as we were falling asleep...

IRIS: Those were some good eel bones.

ME: You said it.

IRIS: That was a funny "cash register."

ME: You're doing air quotes again, aren't you?

On the River

浅草

*When you go to Asakusa you feel that you have shaken
off tomorrow's work.*
   —Saitō Ryokū

ASAKUSA HAS ALWAYS BEEN ONE of the easiest Tokyo neighborhoods to love and one that has fascinated Western tourists. Edward Seidensticker's idiosyncratic (that is, cranky)
history, *Tokyo from Edo to Shōwa,* is essentially a five hundred–page lament about how Asakusa isn't what it used to be
before the fire of 1923.

Don't believe a word of it. Asakusa's striking Kaminarimon
("thunder") Gate still deserves to be the gateway to Tokyo
for any visitor. You can wander the streets south of Sensō-
ji temple for hours, darting in and out of the gaudy tourist
arcade called Nakamise-dōri, get delightfully lost, load up on

souvenirs, and stop off for conveyor belt sushi or tempura (an Asakusa specialty) or an izakaya meal whenever you like.

Asakusa is in the old part of Tokyo, the low city (*shitamachi*), and it's full of faithfully reconstructed historical buildings—reconstructed because Asakusa was destroyed in both 1923 and 1945. Iris loves the place, especially the crowded Nakamise, where she loads up on freshly made rice crackers (*osembei*) and all sorts of unspeakable trinkets: stuffed animals, keychains, stuffed animal keychains. "Asakusa is kind to foreigners...and especially to foreign children," writes Seidensticker. Iris could have told you that.

Not to be outdone in the cuteness department, I bought a purple sleeve for my PASMO transit card. Running perpendicular to Nakamise is a covered shopping arcade called Shin Nakamise-dōri ("New Nakamise"), lined with restaurants and more interesting shops. It's also fun to walk just behind the Nakamise stalls, parallel to the chaos but infinitely quieter, and find the knife shops and stationery stores, the wagashi sweet shops and quirky restaurants like the one specializing in *kamameshi,* steamed rice with flavorings in a little iron pot, a bit like Korean bibimbap.

Walk around Asakusa in the early morning, and you'll see the city yawning and waking up. Few shops, even bakeries and cafes, open in Tokyo before 10 a.m. Visiting insomniacs end up at the Starbucks on Kaminarimon-dōri, which opens at 7 and serves the *hōjicha* latte, a low-caffeine but still addictive beverage of smoky roasted tea and steamed milk.

One day I walked down the covered arcade and stopped into a spice shop called Yagembori, which has specialized in shichimi tōgarashi since 1625. The man behind the counter, a stocky young guy with a mustache, hadn't been working there quite that long.

Shichimi tōgarashi is a blend of seven spices, with ground red chile always prominent. What makes it different from any old chile powder are the other six players: nori flakes, something tangy like dried lemon peel, Sichuan peppercorns (called *sanshō* in Japanese), sesame, hemp seed, and so on. You can buy a little red jar of shichimi tōgarashi at any Japanese grocery, and it will cost a couple of bucks and improve any noodle dish, soup, or beef bowl.

At Yagembori, however, every employee is a professional spice blender. If you have the linguistic chops, you can tell them to throw in a little more sesame or whatever your pleasure. If, like me, you lack the chops, you can just say "spicy." In any case, the counter man scoops individual spices from seven trays into a wooden bowl, stirs it vigorously, and holds it under your nose. You, the customer, swoon. A freshly-mixed packet of Yagembori spice blend is 500 yen, less than a jar of McCormick cinnamon.

At home in Nakano, Iris, who recoils at all things spicy, kept daintily sprinkling shichimi tōgarashi on her rice and eating it two grains at a time. She made me tell and retell the story of how I bought the spice mixture from a grinning shopkeeper who mixed up custom spice blends on the spot. Like so many diners these days, she likes her food to come with a story.

Tokyo has a gaudy replica of the Eiffel Tower called Tokyo

Tower. Constructed in 1958, Tokyo Tower is red and white and looks less like a beloved landmark and more like one of those TV towers you don't want too near your house lest it interfere with your reception. (We didn't have cable when I was growing up, and I'm still bitter.)

Japan has always appropriated its favorite foreign symbols and structures. There are Statue of Liberty replicas all over the country, and one of the most popular attractions for domestic tourists is a faithfully recreated Dutch village called Huis Ten Bosch.

For its latest architectural insanity, however, Tokyo has built something homegrown, ambitious, and mostly just plain huge. The Tokyo SkyTree looks nothing like the Eiffel Tower; it looks like the place a comic book supervillain would mount his death ray. At 634 meters, it's the world's second-tallest freestanding structure after (naturally) a building in Dubai.

When Iris and I stayed in Asakusa in 2010, there was no SkyTree. More to the point, there was no SkyTree merchandise. The shopping arcade of Nakamise-dori has always been Tokyo's gateway to kitschy merchandise, but now it's all SkyTree water bottles, SkyTree cell phone charms, SkyTree hand towels, SkyTree milk caramels. I would bet a hundred dollars you can buy a SkyTree dildo.

One morning I set out into Asakusa at 6 a.m. It was a Saturday, and the streets were empty except for old men strolling and beautiful women bicycling. I wandered along Dembo-in street, just south of the Sensō-ji temple complex, and came to a narrow lane lavishly decorated with streamers in all colors—actually, just the most saturated ones. I couldn't figure out what they were celebrating until I turned around and saw the SkyTree, visible all the way to its base, framed by the cavalcade of corkscrews.

Of course I snapped a picture. But it's hard to find a place to stand in this neighborhood where you *can't* see the SkyTree. It is so out of scale, its design so space-age, that it looks fake, like a plastic model from a 100-yen store.

Usually such a soaring monument is considered an out-of-character pimple for a few years before gaining grudging acceptance and later adulation from people who tell you they loved it all along. When the Eiffel Tower was under construction, Parisian notables considered it a ruinous eyesore. In Seattle, we have a Frank Gehry-designed museum called the Experience Music Project, which looks like brightly colored oatmeal dropped from a height. It's not well-liked, but give it time. As Stewart Brand says in his book *How Buildings Learn,* there are no unloved 100-year-old buildings.

The SkyTree, however, skipped right over its gawky adolescence: locals love it. For two months after it opened in May 2012, tickets were available only by advance purchase to people with Japanese-issued bank cards. It sold out every day. When I talked to people about the SkyTree, they smiled. There was none of the reflexive Japanese "oh, that thing" modesty. The SkyTree stands for the proposition that Japan can still build cool stuff.

I love the SkyTree, too. For something so big, it's playful, almost cuddly, and the builders found a great place to stick it. Er, that didn't sound right. What I mean is: when you come into the city from Narita Airport, you *will* get an eyeful of SkyTree. "Welcome to Tokyo," it says. "Here's something you certainly won't see anywhere else."

In mid-July, the SkyTree started selling same-day tickets to anyone with 2000 yen to spare. Iris and I rode over to SkyTree station on the newly rechristened Tōbu SkyTree line (formerly the Isesaki line). It was a cloudy day—zero chance of a Fuji sighting—and there was no line. The elevator whisked us up 350 meters in seconds. The walls of the SkyTree elevator are opaque and inlaid with brightly colored LED designs. As an acrophobia sufferer, I support this design decision. When we got out on the Tembo Deck, I let Iris wander around while I stayed back from the windows and breathed deeply. Eventually, I was able to peer westward at the view of Asakusa, of Ueno Park, Nakano, and, lurking invisibly behind a wall of suspended water vapor as thick as pudding, Mount Fuji.

I was ready to head home for some comforting udon after ten seconds. However, once you're up on the Tembo Deck, you can drop (maybe "drop" is the wrong word) an additional 1000 yen to go 100 meters higher, to the Tembo Galleria. *If you're going to do this thing, go all the way,* it taunts. Iris talked me into it. This one is a glass elevator, with views through the floor and ceiling. I looked up into the elevator shaft and thought about *Die Hard.*

On Tembo Galleria deck, you emerge at 445 meters and walk the last 5 meters on a sloping pathway curled around the circumference of the structure. You can see this observation deck from the ground, and it looks like a raised eyebrow. It's the SkyTree's most endearing feature; no fascist would construct anything so quirky.

This is exactly what a cranky acrophobe would say, but you don't have to go up the SkyTree to enjoy it. Tokyo is more impressive from the ground than from the air. *Sometimes it's especially impressive below-ground,* I thought, as Iris and I finally caught the train to Nakano and stepped into our favorite basement udon restaurant for steaming bowls of noodles.

Walk fifteen minutes west of Kaminarimon Gate, and you'll see a giant chef's head growing out of a building. This marks the entrance to Kappabashi-dōri, the restaurant supply district.

Kappabashi is written up in most guidebooks as the place to buy the plastic food you see in restaurant windows. This is true, and it's also true that plastic food costs a lot more than real food, which seems only fair, since it's rather more durable. A plate of plastic noodles, for example, costs about $60; a plate of real noodles is more like $6.

But Kappabashi is much more than plastic food. Anything cool you've seen in or around a Tokyo restaurant is for sale here, and you'll recognize tableware, utensils, and more from your meals out. One shop specializes in noren, the curtains flapping in front of restaurant doorways. In summer, many shops sell everything you need to set up your own kakigōri stand: the ice-shaving machine, the syrups and their dispenser, the flower-shaped plastic cups, and the light blue kakigōri advertising banner, emblazoned with the kanji for ice: 氷. A store selling plastic sushi also sold a $200 wall clock with twelve pieces of nigiri sushi instead of numerals.

We even found a shop selling ramen ticket machines. You use the ticket machine in front of the store to select which ticket machine you want to buy. Just kidding.

Most Kappabashi business is wholesale, but retail customers are welcome at every store we visited. My friend Neil is a pastry chef, and he asked us to look for heavy-duty molds for baking *canelé,* an obscure French pastry. They were easy to find and inexpensive, and Neil marveled at the quality. I spent a long time in a store selling Korean tableware, including a huge selection of stone bowls for making dolsot bibimbap, rice with assorted toppings served in a deadly hot stone bowl that crisps the bottom of the rice.

Probably our favorite shop on Kappabashi, however, was Hashito, which sells only chopsticks, from giant sacks of disposable *waribashi* at pennies per unit to handmade artisan pairs for $200 and up.

Before our first trip to Japan, I tried and failed to teach Iris to use chopsticks. We watched YouTube videos and bought snazzy Korean teaching chopsticks with finger loops and rests. No dice; Iris made it through with forks and fingers and the confidence that meant, as a cute American kid, she could get away with the most savage displays of sloppy eating.

Before our month in Tokyo, I gave Iris a pair of kid-sized chopsticks (no loops or training wheels) and a bowl of star anise (easy to pick up) and told her she had to practice for at least five minutes every day before playing video games. There was plenty of grumbling, and it worked. Iris arrived in Tokyo a fluent chopstick user. In a couple of years, I'm going to teach her to drive by turning her loose on *Grand Theft*

Auto.

In Oishinbo: Japanese Cuisine, a teenage girl who has traveled abroad decides that chopsticks are barbaric and that silverware equals civilization. Yamaoka and Kurita take her to visit an artisan who demonstrates the arduous process of making handmade cedar chopsticks. The scene is classically paced ("And now they're done, right?" "Ha ha, not quite yet," ten times), and the girl predictably flings her knife and fork aside by the end. The most expensive chopsticks at Hashito, like high-quality Japanese products in general, are like the ones in Oishinbo: plain and humble, not heavily ornamented. Japanese knives are like this, too; you can certainly buy flashy Damascus steel knives with quilted cocobolo wood handles, but real cooks spend just as much or more on knives that look perfectly ordinary but feel extraordinary.

Iris, who is not known for the subtlety of her aesthetic, bought a pair of chopsticks capped with semiprecious stones. I didn't buy any fancy chopsticks, because I remembered the following scene in Oishinbo, in which Yamaoka and the gang break in their new artisan sticks at a rustic meal. As they finish up, the villain Kaibara Yūzan, who is somehow always invited to these things, demands to see everybody's chopsticks and berates them for eating like cavemen, specifically, letting a whole inch of their chopsticks become food-stained, rather than just the very tips. As if I didn't have enough to worry about.

We were not the first Western tourists to fall in love with Asakusa. A couple from the U.S. spent the summer in Tokyo in 1879. Their names were Ulysses and Julia Grant. The former first couple traveled around Japan but were especially taken with Tokyo and in particular with the low city area around the Sumida River, which runs alongside Asakusa.

In late July, the Grants joined the rest of the city in celebrating the "opening of the Sumida." Like many festivals in Japan, this one involves setting off a shitload of fireworks and stuffing your face with street food, which is usually rare in Tokyo but proliferates wherever people celebrate outdoors. Seidensticker reports:

> The general viewed it in comfort from an aristocratic villa, it being a day when there were still such villas on the river.... Fireworks and crowds got rained upon. All manner of pyrotechnical glories were arranged in red, white, and blue. The general indicated great admiration.... On the whole, the city seems to have loved the general and the general the city.

This celebration survives very much intact, even though it was canceled for about six decades of the twentieth century due to natural disaster, war, and a Sumida fouled with raw sewage. I guess nobody wants to crowd around a river that smells like poop, no matter how many cans of Sapporo you bring with you.

On the last Saturday in July, the Amster-Burtons made like the Grants and headed over to Asakusa to stake out our spot in Sumida River Park to watch the fireworks. We joined over a million other Tokyoites, mostly twentysomethings relaxing on blue tarps with their friends, drinking beer or canned chuhai, and eating street food. To blend in with the locals (not really), Laurie went to the 100-yen store to buy our blue tarp, which was identified on the packaging as a leisure sheet. "Have sex on a leisure sheet" is totally going on my bucket list, albeit purely because of the linguistic connotation, not because of any beneficial feature of the leisure sheet, an extremely thin $1 sheet of plastic. Just call me Leisure Sheet Larry.

Before heading to Asakusa, we bought picnic food at our local 7-Eleven: assorted rice balls, a couple of menchikatsu patties (seasoned ground beef, breaded and fried), crudités, fresh pineapple, and a bag of chocolate cookies. After we spread out our leisure sheet, I bought a giant kakigōri, the shave ice saturated with lemon, melon, cherry, and other lurid fruit syrups, and we settled in to watch the fashion parade.

Forget Harajuku girls. The Sumida fireworks festival offers the most drool-worthy people watching anywhere. Women, and a few men, put on their best summer yukata and parade up and down the banks of the river, and we saw literally thousands of colorful yukata on thousands of beautiful women. Vendors sold *yakisoba* (stir-fried noodles with meat and vegetables), fried chicken, hot dogs on sticks, and okonomiyaki pancakes, and of course you can't pass a summer evening in Tokyo without a kyūri, a Japanese cucumber; at festivals they're briefly marinated with soy sauce and kombu, speared on a chopstick, and kept fresh in lightly salted ice water. To paraphrase George Carlin, if you are a straight man and can watch a woman in a yukata eat a cucumber on a stick without thinking about blow jobs, check your vitals.

I went to the vending machine for water, and when I came back, Iris was gone. "She's over there," said Laurie, rolling her eyes. Iris was, indeed, across the path, on the lap of Naoko, who somehow became Iris's BFF in the space of five minutes. Naoko's yukata was purple and white striped with pink flowers, and she shared her leisure sheet with Takashi, Yūko, and Hanata, all of whom wore stylish civilian garb. I joined them for a while, and we talked about our favorite foods in halting Japanglish, and I drove Iris nuts in classic Dad fashion by asking her questions in Japanese. "Dada, WHY do you keep talking to me in Japanese?" she wailed. I wasn't doing it on purpose, I told her; my brain kept jumping tracks. After I left, reported Iris, they went back to talking about sumo and ninjas and snapping cell phone pictures of each other and giggling.

We didn't get Iris back until after the pyrotechnics were over. Naoko and Hanata took turns hoisting her onto their shoulders for a better view and sometimes carried her off to another section of the park for ten or fifteen minutes at a time. Yes, we let tipsy strangers disappear with our daughter into a crowd of a million people. *That* is Tokyo.

The fireworks, you may have gathered, are a bit beside the point. The show is billed as the most retina-scarring over-the-top fireworks extravaganza imaginable. Two barges operated by different companies drop anchor on adjacent stretches of the Sumida and try to outdo each other in size, volume, and style; the actual show lasts over an hour. "Don't miss the finale," people kept telling us. Well, we couldn't see much through the trees, and what we could see, other than the occasional Pokemon-shaped blast, looked a lot like American fireworks, albeit over a longer duration. The SkyTree, illuminated across the river, was more impressive. Of course, I would go back anytime, perhaps after my second term as president.

Reentry

帰国する

"Places make the best lovers."
—Peter Rees, London city planner, quoted in
Craig Taylor's *Londoners*

IMAGINE, FOR A MOMENT, THE life of a happy baby. Mundane details are anything but mundane; every experience is surprising and mostly delightful. You don't understand how anything works, and you're constantly trying to decipher the processes, customs, and language that govern your existence. This is frustrating and exhilarating, and every small accomplishment produces a rush of pride and an involuntary smile and giggle.

People around you do their best to make sure you're well fed, and every food is delicious and novel. You may feel temporary pain, discomfort, or fear, but you don't yet understand *worry.* You're wrapped in blankets literal and figurative. The world is not only safe, but also tailored for your arrival.

This was my world during our Tokyo summer. Like Tokyo Swayze teaching me to cook okonomiyaki, the entire city was my understanding parent. And then, like real babyhood, it was over too fast. We arrived back in Seattle at 9:30 on a Tuesday morning. Both Laurie and Iris had Aoba Ramen broth stains on their shirts.

Iris has a friend in Seattle, Michael, who lives down the block. He's a smart, introverted kid who likes to start every sentence with "excuse me" and is as adept at dissecting and parrying adult arguments as I was at his age. Whenever he and Iris get together to play, I try to break up the fun before the inevitable dispute over the precise rules of Lego monsters vs. Lego bodybuilders. I always say something stupid like, "Let's end the play date while it's still fun." You can imagine how persuasive this is to two eight-year-olds. They usually respond with something like, "Just ten more hours!"

Now I know exactly how Iris feels, because Tokyo and I ended the play date while it was still fun.

On our first day back, I walked along the left side of the sidewalk, Tokyo-style, and kept bumping into people and murmuring "sumimasen." Iris looked around our apartment and said, "This feels like a hotel." Then she revealed that she'd memorized the long Chūō Rapid announcement, in Japanese, that plays as the train approaches Shinjuku: "The next station is Shinjuku. Transfer here for the Yamanote Line, the Saikyo Line, the Shōnan-Shinjuku Line, the Odakyu line…" She can also do a pitch-perfect impression of the British-accented Shinkansen announcements. We hung Iris's kakigōri banner on our balcony, but it failed to summon an orderly queue of parched tourists.

My sister-in-law Wendy is a gifted book critic. She loves reading about travel and has been known to call a book onto the carpet for "unacknowledged privilege," where the author seems blissfully unaware that they are getting away with something. Stories starring a white guy in Asia are, I suspect, especially susceptible to this syndrome. I hope it's clear that this book is written from a position of acknowledged privilege. For my family, spending a month in Tokyo did not require major sacrifice (well, I did learn a *lot* of kanji), never put us in a dangerous situation, and was basically a way to turn a lot of money into a whole lot of fun and noodles.

When I think about going back to Tokyo, I'm torn. On the one hand, I have a list of restaurants we didn't make it to, and I'm eager to try the fall and winter specials at Hanamaru Udon (beef and burdock! salt-grilled pork and negi!). For that matter, I'd love to spend a good long time in Tokyo during a season that doesn't give me weird heat rashes. (My least favorite place to go in Tokyo was the drugstore: nearly every time I went there, it was to ask where they kept something embarrassing.) Iris would like to catch up with Zen so they can fire more make-believe weapons at each other, and I'd like to get to know Akira and Emi better and try out some of the slang I'm learning from Japanese-language Oishinbo, which presumably makes me sound like an office worker from the nineties. Also, did I mention crispy soup dumplings?

Before we visited Tokyo, Laurie was a Japanese food skeptic. She didn't eat sushi. She was tofuphobic. One day near the end of our trip, she said, "I can't remember why I ever thought I didn't like Japanese food." Now she is a Japanese food snob, observing that Japanese food in Seattle can't compare to what you can get in Tokyo.

I could go back to Tokyo, but not as a baby. I'd have to grow up and form an adult relationship with the city. Vacation Head is an acute disease. It can last a month, but not forever. Every couple happily married after many years will tell you the same story: it's even better now than it was at the beginning, but it took a hell of a lot of work to get here. Forging the same kind of relationship with Tokyo that I have with Laurie seems impossible (for one thing, where would I get a wedding ring big enough to put around the SkyTree?). The alternatives—keeping it casual with the occasional visit or just letting our Tokyo summer amber over into memory— are unsatisfying.

This kind of handwringing is going to earn me a seal of unacknowledged privilege, because I realize that anyone who is in a position to even think about these questions should pat himself on the back and go do something nice for someone else. So let's wrap this up.

The difference between having a relationship with a city and one with a person is that cities are unfailingly polyamorous. Given the means, you can be a Tokyo baby, and I believe you'll love it as much as we did, even if you defy Iris and never set foot in Nakano.

But seriously, you do *not* need to try pachinko.

Bibliography

書誌

THESE BOOKS ABOUT JAPANESE FOOD, culture, language, and travel were indispensable on my journey from knowing nothing about Tokyo to knowing a teeny tiny bit about it.

First, a few books I think everyone heading to Tokyo should read or bring along:

Kariya, Tetsu and Akira Hanasaki. *Oishinbo.* Seven volumes in the *A La Carte* series, published in English by VIZ Media, 2009–2010. There is no greater introduction to the vast world of Japanese cuisine than this eccentric comic series. Begin with the first volume, *Japanese Cuisine,* and see if you aren't hooked.

Tokyo City Atlas. Kodansha, 2012. Even if you bring a smartphone, you'll want to carry this slim book of maps; often one will step up where the other fails.

Robinson, Mark. *Izakaya*. Kodansha, 2008. Eating and drinking at an izakaya is one of the most exuberant food experiences you can have, up there with Spanish tapas and Thai street food. *Izakaya* takes you inside eight great Tokyo izakaya, with recipes, but it's also a history, how-to, and culture guide, with beautiful photos.

Sakamoto, Yukari. *Food Sake Tokyo*. Little Bookroom, 2010. I can't gush enough about this guidebook, which led us to literally dozens of great meals and shops. It's a restaurant guide that also covers department store food shopping, outdoor markets, noodle chains, teahouses, and Tsukiji fish market. If it's in Tokyo and worth eating, it's in this book. The author keeps the book up to date on her blog, foodsaketokyo.wordpress.com.

And the rest:

Akio, Irene. *T is for Tokyo*. Global Directions/Things Asian Press, 2010. A cute children's A-to-Z picture book about Tokyo, with a surprise ending.

Anderson, Tim. *Tune in Tokyo: The Gaijin Diaries*. AmazonEncore, 2011. Anderson's hilarious self-published memoir is more about the author than about Tokyo, but it sure is funny.

Andoh, Elizabeth. *Washoku: Recipes from the Japanese Home Kitchen*. Ten Speed Press, 2005.

Bourdain, Anthony. *A Cook's Tour*. Harper Perennial, 2002. This is going to sound dumb, but I never really understood that Tokyo was a serious food destination until reading the chapter "Tokyo Redux" in this book.

Bunting, Chris. *Drinking Japan*. Tuttle, 2011. An illustrated travel guide to beer, sake, and shōchū establishments throughout Japan.

Carey, Peter. *Wrong About Japan*. Vintage, 2006. A father takes his teenage son on a comic book-inspired trip to Tokyo.

Chavouet, Florent. *Tokyo on Foot*. Tuttle, 2011. A lavishly hand-illustrated walk through Tokyo neighborhoods by a French artist.

Davidson, Cathy. *36 Views of Mount Fuji*. Duke University Press, 2006.

Dibble, Craig. *Real Life Japanese Food*. Unicom, 2002. This weird and hard-to-find book (it's not on Amazon, as far as I can tell) is a Japanese language course centered entirely around food. Highly recommended if you can turn one up.

Dunlop, Fuchsia. *Every Grain of Rice*. W.W. Norton, 2013. Includes a great recipe for smacked cucumber salad, similar to the one we ate at the crispy soup dumpling restaurant in Nakano.

Garcia, Héctor. *A Geek in Japan*. Tuttle, 2011. An illustrated introduction to geeky pursuits in Japan, especially manga, anime, and electronics.

Gibson, William. *Pattern Recognition*. Putnam, 2005. I don't think there's any writer I envy more than Gibson, whose descriptions of street-level Shibuya in this novel will be painfully nostalgic to anyone who has been there.

Gibson, William. *Distrust That Particular Flavor*. Putnam,

2012. Includes a couple of short nonfiction essays about Tokyo.

Grescoe, Taras. *Straphanger: Saving Our Cities and Ourselves from the Automobile*. Times Books, 2012. Includes an astonishing chapter about the scale and operation of the Tokyo train system.

Heisig, James. *Remembering the Kanji, Volume 1*. University of Hawaii Press, 2011. Probably the best way to learn kanji as an adult. Guaranteed to drive you crazy nevertheless.

Iyer, Pico. *The Lady and the Monk*. Vintage, 1992. A sentimental account of a year spent falling in love with Kyoto and a woman. Iyer went looking for a quiet and contemplative Japan very different from mine, and found it, but we share an appreciation for the way Japan can make an adult feel like a happy baby.

Kaneko, Amy. *Let's Cook Japanese Food*. Chronicle, 2007. If you've never cooked Japanese food at home before, I'd start with this simple and very Westernized book, then move on to a cookbook by Andoh, Kurihara, Tsuji, or Kobayashi.

Kashiba, Shiro. *Shiro: Wit, Wisdom and Recipes from a Sushi Pioneer*. Chin Music Press, 2011. As much memoir as cookbook, very much worth reading even if you have no plans to make sushi at home.

Kawabata, Yasunari. *The Scarlet Gang of Asakusa*. University of California Press, 2005. A bizarre picaresque novel set in Roaring Twenties Asakusa. I've always wanted to throw around the term "picaresque"; goal achieved.

Kerr, Alex. *Lost Japan*. Lonely Planet, 2009. And *Dogs and*

Demons. Hill and Wang, 2002. This pair of controversial books by Kerr, a Westerner who has lived in Japan most of his life, explore the dark side of Japanese society. Worth reading for several reasons: Kerr is a great writer; he has some amazing stories; and he is so negative about Japan that you'll get the impression that the entire country is corrupt, despondent, and cemented over. Then, when you visit, your expectations can't help but be exceeded.

Kobayashi, Kentaro. *Donburi Mania*. Vertical, 2009. A delightful little cookbook of rice bowl dishes. I was planning to email the author and ask if we could meet up in Tokyo; it turns out he's a celebrity chef whose face I kept seeing on posters at bookstores.

Kurihara, Harumi. *Harumi's Japanese Home Cooking*. HP Trade, 2007.

Matsushima, Kimiko. *Ramen, Udon, Soba*. Amazon Digital Services, 2012. A short, inexpensive electronic cookbook full of very authentic Japanese noodle recipes.

Nguyen, Andrea. *Asian Tofu*. Ten Speed Press, 2012.

Ono, Tadashi and Harris Salat. *Japanese Hot Pots*. Ten Speed Press, 2009.

Peters, Mark. *Japan Dreams*. CreateSpace, 2010. While researching this book, I had all of my prejudices about self-publishing shattered. *Japan Dreams* is beautifully written, weird, sexy, and full of smart observations. Highly recommended.

Pond, Karen. *Getting Genki in Japan*. Tuttle, 2012. A comic memoir in the Erma Bombeck mold by an American woman trying to figure out how Tokyo works.

Presser, Brandon. *Lonely Planet: Tokyo Encounter*. Lonely Planet, 2012. A good choice for a small, general-purpose guidebook.

Reid, T.R. *Confucius Lives Next Door*. Vintage, 2000. Reid tries to construct a thesis about Asian societies that has something to do with Confucianism. I never really understood the argument, but there are lots of great stories about Tokyo and other Asian cities in here.

Renn, Diana. *Tokyo Heist*. Viking Juvenile, 2012. A young adult mystery set in Seattle and Tokyo. Includes the great line, "I'm being grounded? For going to Asakusa?"

Reynolds, Betty. *Squeamish about Sushi*. Tuttle, 2006. And *Clueless in Tokyo*. Tuttle, 1997. A pair of illustrated guides to things you'll see in Tokyo on your plate and otherwise. Reynolds has a colorful watercolor style that is very easy to like.

Samuels, Debra. *My Japanese Table*. Tuttle, 2011.

Satterwhite, Robb. *What's What in Japanese Restaurants*. Kodansha, 2011. If you're nervous about stepping into the kind of Tokyo restaurants I visited, get this book, which walks you through the different types of restaurants you'll find, how to navigate them, and what you'll find on the menu (in Japanese, English, and romanized Japanese).

Seidensticker, Edward. *Tokyo: From Edo to Shōwa*. Tuttle, 2010. An opinionated and readable history of Tokyo.

Steinberger, Amy. *Japan Ai* (日本愛). Go! Comi, 2007. A fun, brief, illustrated memoir about an American woman taking her first trip to Japan.

Tsuji, Shizuo. *Japanese Cooking: A Simple Art*. Kodansha,

2005. First published in 1980, this is still the best English-language Japanese cookbook you can buy.

Williamson, Kate. *A Year in Japan.* Princeton Architectural Press, 2006. Another swoony Kyoto memoir, this one lovingly illustrated. Worth it just for Williamson's visual catalogs of tenugui and socks. Incidentally, the author's other memoir, *At a Crossroads,* has nothing to do with Japan but is one of my all-time favorite books.

And a handful of movies:

The Fast and the Furious: Tokyo Drift. 2006. Seriously, this movie is so great.

Jiro Dreams of Sushi. 2011.

Lost in Translation. 2003.

Walk Don't Run. 1966. This screwball comedy set at the 1964 Tokyo Olympics was Cary Grant's final film. Pretty funny, and filmed on location in Shimbashi.

Acknowledgments

謝辞

THIS BOOK FORCED ITSELF OUT of me in a messy Alien-like process visible only to the unlucky patrons of the cafes where it was written: Remedy Teas in Seattle and the Starbucks on Nakano-dōri in Nakano, Tokyo.

Becky Selengut made me take the book further than I'd anticipated. Without Becky's influence, you would have just finished a rambling collection of restaurant reviews. Becky, I'm sorry it's not the graphic novel you wanted. Maybe next time. Becky is the author of the sustainable seafood cookbook *Good Fish*, but never once castigated me for the unsustainable seafood I ate in Japan. Buy her book already.

Molly Wizenberg read drafts and made comments and was there to answer my most needy questions at any time, even though she was writing her own book, opening a restaurant, and having a baby. Nobody has a higher tolerance for my terrible jokes than Molly. It's a little disturbing. Buy her book, *A Homemade Life,* too.

When I thought the manuscript was finished and error-free, I sent it to copy editor Janet Majure (janetmajure.com), who found over five hundred remaining typos, ugly sentences, and inconsistencies. Any remaining errors are mine. If you need a copy editor for your book or any writing project, hire Janet.

Tokyoites Shirley Karasawa (who teaches Japanese home cooking on her blog, lovelylanvin.com) and Yukari Sakamoto (who blogs at foodsaketokyo.wordpress.com) helped me get the Japanese words right. Shirley also teaches Japanese cooking classes in Seattle; Yukari leads food-focused walking tours in Tokyo. Recommended!

Thank you to Akira and Emi, our best friends in Japan. Composing emails to them in Japanese feels exactly like aerobic exercise: I break into a sweat, but then, when I'm done, wow! I wrote a whole email in Japanese! I'm still kind of amazed that we were able to successfully meet with them in the same place at the same time; credit this to Akira's bilingualism.

CL Smith designed the cover. You can hire him at humblenations.com. Iris would like you to know that she thinks the octopus looks evil and would have preferred a cute plush octopus.

At my day job, I write a personal finance column. My colleague Wade Pfau is a retirement planning expert and an economics professor at a Tokyo university. I call on him often for a quote for my column, and he and his family were equally generous with their time in Tokyo.

Kate Johnson came all the way from Chiba to the west

side, twice, to see us, took us to a great restaurant in Shibuya, and introduced Iris and me to this amazing toy where you make candy sushi from scratch. The results are as beautiful as they are inedible. Thank you, Kate!

Elizabeth Andoh's cooking classes are legendary, and I was lucky enough to experience two of them in the same month. Her cookbooks are superb; my favorite is *Washoku*. Find her classes at tasteofculture.com.

As with *Hungry Monkey*, many of the best jokes in this book and none of the worst were written by my friend and joke doctor, Dan Shiovitz. You know how sometimes you meet someone who seems too good-looking to be working a normal job? Dan's like that, only with comedy.

Neil Robertson, pastry chef and Japanophile, alerted us to numerous important pâtisseries, including Aigre-Douce.

Rachael Hutchings, blogger at LaFujiMama.com and co-host of the Miso Hungry podcast, read the manuscript and pointed out many instances where my understanding of Japanese food was less than stellar. She also invited me onto her show to talk about Tokyo supermarkets, and gathering my thoughts for that episode did a lot to improve the supermarket chapter. You can listen to me ramble here: goo.gl/aCnjG

The Usui family of Saitama-ken welcomed us into their home for an afternoon, cooked us an amazing meal, and gave us a couple of memorable restaurant recommendations. Their three kids treated Iris like a best friend from the moment they met.

Thank you to Mac, our apartment manager, and to Zen, Makoto, and Amy, our neighbors. If you're looking for a vacation rental in Tokyo, do not hesitate to use LiveInAsia.com.

In the acknowledgements of my last book, I referred to my family, Laurie and Iris, as "extremely high-quality." This turned out to be a rank understatement. Can you imagine spending a month with *your* family in a 260-square-foot apartment without any murders? Thanks also to my parents, Judy and Richard Amster, who have always been my biggest boosters and have almost never criticized my not-very-moneymaking lifestyle. Writing books is almost as lucrative as playing pachinko, but a lot more fun.

Creating an ebook that mixes English and Japanese alphabets is a real caution. Thanks to Alberto Pettari and Liza Daly for the advice and tools that made it possible. Neil deMause answered my arcane Adobe InDesign questions. Beta testers included Josh Giesbrecht, Gunther Schmidl, Wendy Burton, Justin de Vesine, John Cater, and Tara C. of Kobo technical support.

The production budget for this book came from 381 backers on Kickstarter. It's an incredible honor that hundreds of people from all over the world decided this was a good use of their money. Backers include:

Adrian Drake; Agatha Khishchenko; Alexander Y. Hawson, M.D.; Allen Garvin; Alon Takeuchi; Amanda Powter; Amanda Sargent; Amber Andersen; Amy Plank; Andrea Arnold; Andrew Duff; Anita and Cameron Crotty; Ann Bjorseth; Aoi Ninami; Betty and Dick Balcomb; Brad Mohr; Bruce and Susan Burton; Bruce Ryan; C Milne; Caroline Cummins; Chris Phelps; Christine Li; Chuck Nordhoff; Corinne Burger; Culinate; Cynthia Nims; Dan Shiovitz; Darsa Morrow; David Dadekian; David Glasser; David Mahashin; Dawn, Eric, and Ian Wright; Debbie Jeske; Dirk Elmendorf; Don Lee; Doug

Jones; Emiko Freund; Emily Short; Florentyna Leow (Furo-chan); Glenn Fleishman; Helen Rennie; Henry H Lo, Lorna Yee, and Weston Lo; Hsiao-Ching Chou; Jacqueline L. Ash-well; James Kyoon Yun; James Whetzel; Jamison Moore; Jay Friedman; Jennifer and Greg Barnes; Jess Higgins; Jodi from MI; Joe "Linja" Lin; Jon Rosebaugh; Josie Paras; Judy and Richard Amster; Justin de Vesine; Kairu Yao; Kathleen Burton McDade; Katie Briggs; Kelly Samek; Kim Foster; Kristy Hogue; Lara Ferroni; Larry, Kristen, and Julia Liang; Laura Hooning; Laura Phillips; Lauren E. Cohn; Lauren Edlund; Laurent B. Sauvageau; Lily Yu; Liza Daly; Lizz Zitron; Marius Müller; Mark Musante; Masato Taniguchi; Matt Treiber; Matthew Murray; Megan Tortora; Meghan Feuk; Michael Bourret; Michael Burton; Michael Kitces; MK Carroll; Molly Wizenberg; N. Segovia; Nagayoshi Makoto, Amy, and Zen; Nancy Leson; Nathalie Nasr; Neil deMause; Neil K. Guy; Pat Tanumihardja; Patrick Cheung; Phillip Harris; Pia Thomas; Poh Ling Ng; Priya and Veena Mishra; Rachael Hutchings; Randy Thomson; Rebekah Denn; Robert Musser; Robin Wehl Martin; Roll with Jen; Rowena Fernando-Li; Ryan Franson; Samantha Koss; Sarah H.; Shannon; Sonoko Sakai; Stacy Cowley; Steve Kang; Steve Phifer; Steven Haryanto; Storme Winfield; Susan MacCulloch; Susann Rutledge; Svenssons; Talia Lynch; Tami Parr; Tatsuya Wagatsuma; Thanh P. L. L.; The Laney Family; Therese R. Harris; Wade and Joseph Pfau; Wendy Burton; Yuichi Miyakawa; and Yuki Caldwell.

Finally, thank you to the 30-odd million people of the world's greatest city, for the best month of my life.

ABOUT THE AUTHOR

Matthew Amster-Burton has written about food for Gourmet, the Seattle Times, and the Wall Street Journal, and has been featured in *Best Food Writing* five times. Cohost of the hit podcast Spilled Milk, Matthew lives with his family in Seattle but would rather be eating crispy soup dumplings in Nakano. For photos, visit prettygoodnumberone.com.

1B/170/P